ISBN 978-0-902869-89-9
Published by Socialist Resistance
Printed by Lightning Source
Designed by Ed Fredenburgh

RESPECT: DOCUMENTS OF THE CRISIS

RESPECT: DOCUMENTS OF THE CRISIS

George Galloway, Salma Yaqoob, Alan Thornett and others

EDITED BY FRED LEPLAT

A SOCIALIST RESISTANCE PAMPHLET

CONTENTS

INTRODUCTION

Respect as it was originally constructed – as an alliance primarily between the SWP and George Galloway – is dead. The challenge that Socialist Resistance is now committing itself to is to build Respect Renewal in a way that takes the best from Respect mark 1 while learning from its failures and difficulties.

Respect stood on the gains of the anti-globalisation and anti-war movements, and on the fact that the anti-war movement had begun to build among sections of Muslim communities who had not previously engaged with British politics. Respect Renewal should continue that work.

The opportunities to build such an alternative remain very strong. Brown's honeymoon was short-lived, and increasing numbers are recognising what we have always argued – that you couldn't put a cigarette paper between him and his predecessor. The debate in the trade unions about a political alternative is deepening – and the failure of the hoped-for winter of discontent will probably increase the prominence of this issue amongst activists. Organisations like the CPB, who had continued to place their hope in the resurgence of the Labour Left, are beginning to change their view.

The political context for building an alternative is strengthened, although some will undoubtedly be demoralised, especially in the short term, by the split.

But the Socialist Workers Party is painting a dishonest picture of what lies behind the division within Respect. They claim that they are the left in the split and everyone else is on the right (or is naively misguided, which is just as insulting). They repeat their disgraceful attacks on the Scottish Socialist Party, and by implication make comparison between those who support Respect Renewal with those in Rifondazione who have backed Italian Prime Minister Prodi in sending troops to Afghanistan. Such comparisons are ridiculous.

Disregarding the grandiose comparisons with the splits between the Mensheviks and the Bolsheviks for the delusions they are, this pamphlet shows the political positions of those the SWP would paint as "the right".

It makes clear that all those centrally involved in Respect Renewal are committed to building a socialist alternative to the left of new Labour. It shows that the emotive charge of witch hunting was a diversion from the real debate – which was about the way forward for Respect – and a device to line up SWP members behind their leadership.

The SWP claim that they wanted to challenge the idea that Respect should only be an electoral machine. But this is not the position put forward by anyone here – or as far as we are aware anyone supporting Respect Renewal. It is, however, a position put forward by the SWP in a number of internal communications with their own members – communications that escaped into the blogosphere.

Socialist Resistance has consistently argued for a different model of Respect – for Respect as a party, not a coalition. Such a model puts demands on revolutionaries operating within such a broad party – particularly when they are members of by far the largest group on the far left.

The SWP didn't want to pay the price of fully committing themselves to Respect, and instead invented "the united front of a special type" notion, which allowed them to prioritise their own interests over building the broader organisation. This acted as a barrier to Respect developing a healthy internal life in a way that was attractive to newly radicalising forces.

There has been more political debate since George Galloway wrote his letter in August than during the previous years of Respect's existence. That political debate has seen some of the contributors here, who previously supported the coalition model, now arguing that it is time for a new party.

Not all the contributions we print here are from Socialist Resistance supporters, of course. But we think and hope that by publishing this collection we can contribute to an important debate, and thus help to build a socialist alternative to the ravages of war and neo-liberalism. ∎

COUNTDOWN TO THE CRISIS

Saturday 19 August
SWP caucus receives report that George Galloway is considering writing something about the situation in Respect. Immediate SWP reaction is that if it's an attack on them, it would be time to "go nuclear".

Thursday 23 August
George Galloway sends letter to NC members.

23 August—7 September
SWP delegation meets with Galloway, Salma Yaqoob and others to discuss Galloway letter. SWP believes it is a big attack on them. Nothing is resolved.

Friday 7 September
Galloway is denounced at all-London meeting of SWP members.

23 August—21 September
Contributions are written by Salma Yaqoob and Alan Thornett and one from John Rees and Elaine Graham Leigh. The latter is hostile and defensive. Internally SWP hold a series of aggregate meetings in which GG and SY are accused of communalism.

CONTINUED ON PAGE 5

IT WAS THE BEST OF TIMES, IT WAS THE WORST OF TIMES

George Galloway, letter to Respect National Council

The Shadwell by-election victory has stunned the New Labour establishment, turned the tide in Tower Hamlets and opened up the real possibility of winning two parliamentary seats in East London which, together with the potential gain in Birmingham, would make us the most successful left-wing party in British history.

New Labour's decision to try to rehabilitate Michael Keith – the former leader of Tower Hamlets council who we first defeated last year – raised the stakes in this election enormously. A victory for him in a ward where we had all three councillors would have thrown us into a grave crisis. Instead, it is Labour that is suffering shattering demoralisation and we are enjoying a post-Shadwell bounce.

Ealing Southall, on the other hand, just a few weeks before, marked the lowest point in Respect's three-year history. The failure to harvest even the vote we had secured in just one ward of the constituency in the local elections 12 months earlier, was a sharp reminder that what goes up can come down, and should shatter any complacency about the London elections next May.

It is clear to everyone, if we are honest, that Respect is not punching its weight in British politics, and has not fulfilled its potential, either in terms of votes consistently gained, members recruited, or fighting funds raised. The primary reasons for this are not objective circumstances, but internal problems of our own making.

The conditions for Respect to grow strongly obtain in just the same way as they did when we first launched the organisation and had our historic breakthrough in 2005.

Anyone who was at the 1000-strong street celebration after the victory in Shadwell will attest that the idea of Respect remains very much alive and, as Jim Fitzpatrick MP said in Tribune, it's clear that "the Iraq war hasn't gone away".

Michael Lavalette's advancing position in Preston shows what can be done with imaginative and dedicated work. In Bristol around Jerry Hicks, and in Sheffield around Maxine Bowler, we have placed ourselves in pole position to enter the council chamber. But to achieve that we must recognise our serious internal weaknesses, which are becoming more apparent and which threaten to derail the whole project.

Membership

Despite being a rather well known political brand, our membership has not grown. And in some areas it has gone into a steep decline. Whole areas of the country are effectively moribund as far as Respect activity is concerned. In some weeks there is not a single Respect activity anywhere in the country advertised in our media. No systematic effort has been able to be mounted – in fact, a major effort had to be launched to get back to the levels of membership we had, despite electoral successes, widespread publicity, and the continuing absence of any serious rival on the left. This has left a small core of activists to shoulder burden after burden without much in the way of support from the centre, leading to exhaustion and enervation.

Fundraising

This is all but non-existent. We have stumbled from one financial crisis to another. And with the prospect of an early general election, we are simply unable to challenge the major parties in our key constituencies. None of the Respect staff appears to have been tasked with either membership or fundraising responsibilities. Or if they have it isn't working. There is a deep-seated culture of amateurism and irresponsibility on the question of money. Activities are not properly budgeted and even where budgets are set they are not adhered to. Take, for example, the Fighting Unions Conference which was full to the rafters but still managed to lose £5000. The intervention at Pride, where we gave away merchandise rather than sold it, lost £2000.

It is a moot point whether the turn to building Fighting Unions, which occupied the National Office for four months, was the correct prioritisation of slender resources, following our breakthroughs at the local elections last year. What is not moot is that

CONTINUED FROM PAGE 3

Saturday 22 September
National Council meeting. SWP members denounce George Galloway. He walks out of meeting saying he will resign from the NC and will not stand in the election. He is persuaded to go back. Afterwards sections of his proposals adopted unanimously. Meeting adjourned until September 29 to complete business.

Saturday 29 September
National Council. Motion to urge Galloway to reconsider and resume candidacy moved by SWP member and carried unanimously. Debate over formula for National Organiser and unanimous agreement on formula. Galloway proposes Nick Wrack for the job as acceptable to both sides of NC.

Tuesday 30 September
SWP National council meets. Opposition develops inside SWP to the actions of the leadership in all this.

Monday 8 October
Nick Wrack told by SWP he is not acceptable to them as National Organiser as he has political differences with them over Respect.

Wednesday 10 October
Alan Thornett proposes

CONTINUED ON PAGE 7

mismanagement turned an event which ought to have been a money-spinner into a money-loser.

Equally the Pride intervention, which occupied a great deal of the organisation's time (I personally was telephoned three times to be asked if I would make it, and others report similar pressure) can be compared to the total lack of a presence at the Barking Mela last weekend – the biggest in Europe – or the minimal campaigning presence at the recent London Latin American festival. Again, while it is arguable that Pride was the priority, what is not arguable is that fundraising at the event should have been included in the plan.

Further, what ought to have been the unalloyed success of the Pride intervention was seriously marred. Instead of a simple encouragement for members to attend – with a logical emphasis on LGBT members and young people – several members in elected office were subjected to a high-handed "instruction" from the national office to take part. It appeared to them to be some kind of misplaced test of their commitment to the equality programme of the organisation. This is frankly absurd. There are LGBT people who don't feel comfortable being on a float on a parade. It would be a serious mistake to read off someone's commitment to equality from their willingness to be dancing on the back of a truck on the Pride parade.

Having done that and spent £2,000, there was no effort to publicise our intervention externally by ensuring that all the relevant media and organisations were made aware that we were the only political party to have a float on the parade.

Staffing

This is a mystery to me and others. People pop up as staff members in jobs which have not been advertised, for which there have been no interviews, and whose job descriptions are unclear and certainly unpublished. One staff member was appointed at a meeting at which that same staff member was present, making it obviously embarrassing for anyone to query whether they were the right person for the job, whether they could be afforded, or why the job should go to them rather than someone else. This unnecessarily poor management leads to tensions, even animosity and the suspicion that staff are recruited for their political opinions on internal matters rather than on a proper basis. Sometimes the conduct of some staff buttresses this suspicion. For example, at the selection meeting for our Shadwell candidate, two members of staff were openly proselytising for one candidate and against another – including heckling – even after the decision had been taken. This undoubtedly contributed to the exceedingly poor involvement of the wider membership in the subsequent election. No paid member of staff attended the Shadwell victory celebrations, and when I asked one of them if they would be attending, I was told "No, I'll be watching the football". This was noticed widely by the activists who were present at the celebration and commented upon it. It is again bad management to allow such culture and practices to proliferate.

Internal relations

There is a custom of anathematisation in the organisation which is deeply unhealthy and has been the ruin of many a left-wing group before us. This began with Salma Yaqoob, once one of our star turns, promoted on virtually every platform, and who is responsible for some of the greatest election victories (and near misses) during our era. Now she has been airbrushed from our history at just the time when she is becoming a regular feature on the national media and her impact on the politics of Britain's second city has never been higher.

There appears to be no plan to rescue her from this perdition, indeed every sign that her internal exile is a fixture. This is intolerable and must end now. Whatever personal differences may exist between leading members, the rest of us cannot allow Respect to be hobbled in this way. We are not over-endowed with national figures.

Decision making and implementation

There is a marked tendency for decisions made at the National Council, or avenues signposted for exploration, to be left to wither on the vine if they are not deemed to meet priorities (which themselves are not agreed). For example, there was a very useful discussion at the last National Council on what initiatives we should explore following Brown's succession

CONTINUED FROM PAGE 5

that NC decision to appoint Nick Wrack is implemented forthwith. Nick Wrack told by SWP to withdraw his name.

Friday 12 October
Nick Wrack expelled from SWP. Kevin Ovenden and Rob Hoveman receive an ultimatum to resign from their posts in Galloway's office or face expulsion from SWP.

Sunday 14 October
20 members of National Council circulate letter supporting Nick Wrack as candidate for national organiser.
Rob Hoveman and Kevin Ovenden expelled from SWP.

Monday 15 October
Respect officers meeting at which there is only one candidate for national organiser, Nick Wrack. Officers meeting votes not to appoint – overturning decision of National Council. Linda Smith proposes additions to CAC which are not agreed.

Tuesday 16 October
CAC meeting. Linda Smith argues the CAC is unconstitutional as its membership not agreed by NC. Linda asks for membership records and financial contributions behind

CONTINUED ON PAGE 9

and the then anticipated failure of the McDonnell campaign to get out of the starting gate. Among the varied suggestions were some seeking to cohere wider progressive opinion around a minimal five point programme; approaching McDonnell to organise an open meeting in Parliament; seeking a joint conference with the RMT, CPB, Labour left and others; and organising a people's march to London as an agitational vehicle for rallying forces and struggles against the Brown government. None of these have been seriously followed up. The overall emphasis – that the departure of Blair and the failure of the Labour left's strategy opened up possibilities for us both to build Respect directly and to place it at the centre of a progressive realignment – was allowed to run into the ground.

Building the organisation

We must be much more systematic in building Respect's profile in the wider arenas our members are active in. There is no question that struggles such as Stop the War, Defend Council Housing, anti-racist campaigns, activity around trade union disputes and so on are the lifeblood of a progressive political force such as ourselves. But the great lesson of the Stop the War movement in 2003 was that these movements do not automatically give rise to a force that can punch through on the political scene. That requires – as it did when we founded Respect – patient, detailed work and single-mindedness about ensuring that Respect grows out of the wider radical milieu.

Two of our outstanding members are at the helm of Defend Council Housing; many of our members are active in it in their localities. Yet as an organisation we have done far too little to raise the Respect banner inside the campaign and, to put it bluntly, cash in on the work our activists have put in and the turmoil the campaign has caused among disaffected Labour councillors and Labour-supporting tenants and trade unionists.

At the successful Stop the War demonstration outside the Labour Party conference in Manchester in September last year, the nationally produced propaganda was for the Fighting Unions conference. It was thanks only to the Manchester comrades that we had a tabloid promoting Respect as a political formation. It was again thanks to the Manchester comrades that we had such a publication for the protest outside Brown's coronation.

In every area of activity we need to encourage in our members a focus on recruitment, fundraising, establishing the profile of our candidates and unashamedly promoting Respect as the critical force in the wider reconstitution of the progressive and socialist movement.

Internal selections

Then there is the practice of the creation of false dichotomies between candidates for internal elections. Neither Oliur Rahman nor Abjul Miah nor Haroon Miah is Karl Liebknecht. And Sultana Begum is not Rosa Luxemburg. Yet in internal election contests which these four contested in Tower Hamlets, the divisions between them were deliberately and artificially exaggerated, and members mobilised about "principles" which never were. This has led to deep and lasting divisions which show no signs of healing in the current atmosphere. So we must make a new atmosphere. If we are to rally to win the prize of a seat on the GLA, and three members of parliament, we must start right now.

Relations between leading figures in Respect are at an all-time low and this must be addressed. I have proposals to make which are not aimed at a change of political line, still less an attack on any organisation or section within Respect. They are aimed at placing us on an election war-footing, closing the chasm which has been caused to develop between leading members, together with an emergency fundraising and membership drive to facilitate our forthcoming electoral challenges. Business as usual will not do and everyone in their heart knows this.

The crossroads at which we now stand can take us down either the Shadwell route or the road to Southall.

Instead of three MPs and a presence on the GLA, we could have no MPs and no one on the GLA by this time next year. A few honest moments' thought should suffice to calibrate where that would leave us. Oblivion.

CONTINUED FROM PAGE 7

student delegation: these could not be produced. Meeting precedes Tower Hamlets branch meeting; breaks up in disarray.

Wednesday 17 October
Linda Smith sends to national office a letter for circulation, recalling National Council for October 28. Letter is not circulated for some days; Rees disputes her right to call meeting.

Thursday 18 October
Tower Hamlets committee meeting votes to reconvene members meeting on October 25. SWP walk out.
John Rees circulates through Respect a factional "transcript" of Tower Hamlets committee meeting.

Monday 22 October
John Rees rings Alan Thornett at 9pm to ask if it's correct that a document critical of the SWP is being prepared. Alan confirms it is correct. When asked if it would be signed by many members of the National Council, Alan confirms it would be. John Rees's response is, "in that case, the SWP might as well call it a day". Alan asks, "Do you mean you would walk away from Respect?" John Rees replies, "What would be the point, any more?"

CONTINUED ON PAGE 11

I cannot imagine that any member of the National Council wants to see us arrive at the destination where now lies the wreck of left-wing politics in Scotland, and so I hope that these proposals will be considered with the best interests of the Respect project uppermost in our minds.

A way forward

It is abundantly clear for a variety of reasons that the leadership team must be strengthened and all talents mustered. I therefore propose the creation of a new high-powered elections committee whose task would be to rapidly evaluate our election strengths and weaknesses, proposed target seats, supervise the selection of candidates – national and local – and spearhead a national membership and fundraising drive. This committee must comprise the leading members of Respect, including Salma, Linda Smith, Yvonne Ridley, Abjol Miah (as the leader of our 11 councillors in the central election battleground of Tower Hamlets), me, Lindsey German, Alan Thornett, Nick Wrack as well as the National Secretary.

I also propose a crucial new post of National Organiser, preferably full-time, whose task would be the aforementioned re-organisation and re-energising of the key clusters of Respect support and the encouragement of members everywhere. This position would sit alongside the position of National Secretary. It must be advertised and subject to competitive interview overseen by the elections committee.

While this document may seem stark in black and white, it reflects a widespread feeling which has surfaced in various ways – including at the National Council – and it is clear that the status quo, or minor tinkering, are not options. Time is short, renovation is urgently required and we must start the process now.

George Galloway MP

GEORGE GALLOWAY'S LETTER – WHERE WE STAND

Alan Thornett and John Lister

This is the text we are submitting to the Respect National Council (NC) tomorrow. It is not a voting text but a contribution to the discussion. We will also be putting a resolution to the meeting tomorrow which will be for voting. We will send it out later

---

We welcome the issues raised by the letter George Galloway has sent to the Respect NC, which in effect opens the pre-conference discussion for the Respect conference in November. In fact we have been raising many of the issues ourselves. Some of them we raised at the Respect conference last year. Now Salma Yaqoob, too, has submitted a strong statement echoing similar core points to those raised by George.

We are aware that there has been a discussion between the SWP and George Galloway and others over the letter, and that there is a wider and escalating debate taking place around it. There is a dangerous dynamic to this debate, in which we understand some people have tried to reject the substantial issues raised in George Galloway's letter, by presenting it as a challenge to working class politics in

CONTINUED FROM PAGE 9

Tuesday 23 October
Socialist Worker appears with editorial attacking Galloway and supporters.

Wednesday 24 October
Respect at Crossroads document sent by Linda Smith for circulation to membership. Alan Thornett phones John Rees to ask for a meeting between the two sides. John Rees agrees to meet the following day (Thursday 25 October) to discuss an "amicable separation".

Thursday 25 October
The first meeting between the SWP and representatives of 19 non-SWP members of the Respect National Council, facilitated by a mutual friend. After lengthy discussion there is no agreement on a formula – only on the desirability of such a separation.
Tower Hamlets members' meeting breaks up without agreeing Conference delegates.
Four Tower Hamlets councillors issue press release resigning the Respect whip and attacking Abjol Miah. George Galloway appears on Question Time: internal situation not raised.

CONTINUED ON PAGE 13

Respect, and accusing him – and anyone supporting his criticisms – of adopting what are termed "communalist" politics. Although we have only been marginally involved in this debate, we are very concerned that this line of argument has been raised – it is one which could divide Respect if it is pursued.

Salma's text very capably rebuts any allegation of "communalism". But the clandestine debate has always been a false one, because there are actually no communalist politics, or anything close to it, in George's letter. On the contrary it is an argument for the building of a broad-based organisation more effectively than in the past.

In our view any attempt to use this or other diversionary issues to divert from the valid critique which George Galloway has raised over the situation in Respect, can only undermine future prospects for building it as a broad-based left alternative to New Labour.

Many of George's points are valid and merit a serious and constructive response. In particular we agree with him on the following:

1 There is going to be an early general election – either in the autumn of this year or in the spring of next year. Brown is likely to take advantage of this favourable situation – the crisis of the Tories and the Brown bounce – particularly since it might not last long.

2 Yet Southall demonstrated – if demonstration was needed – that Respect is in no shape to effectively fight an election. Its membership has indeed declined and many of its branches are moribund. The lesson from Southall is that Respect cannot succeed in a new constituency unless it has built a base in that constituency well in advance.

3 The objective conditions which produced Respect, and the space to the left of Labour, remains in full force, as shown by the Shadwell result. Brown leads a right-wing, anti-working class, neoliberal government, which has continued the Blairite relationship with the employers, and is even more hostile to the unions, as his pay freeze makes clear. His scandalous appointment of Digby Jones and other right-wing Tories makes this clear enough. Brown is worse than Blair on civil rights and is equally supportive of US imperialism and its wars. Trident will be replaced just the same.

4 Despite the politics of new Labour, Respect has not fulfilled its potential politically or organisationally. We have long said that a membership of 2,000 or so, for an organisation with a Westminster MP, a presence in local government, and remarkable name recognition, is ridiculously low. Membership has declined from 5,000 in 2005 – an awkward fact that was denied, rather than addressed, at the last conference. The potential for development has been shown, however, in key localities, not only in East London but in Preston, Birmingham and

Sheffield for example, as George's letter and Salma point out.

Respect needs to build itself as a national organisation. This means a stronger national profile and much more attention to building local branches. It needs effective fundraising.

In our view in the longer term the strategic issue is whether Respect should be a political party or a loose coalition. We have argued that the loose coalition model – or "united front of a special kind" or whatever – does not work. We believe that challenging for political power taking on all other political parties and dealing with all the problems that arise needs the structures of a political party: This does not mean that we believe Respect is, or could sensibly be declared to be, a party in any sense at the present time. A process of development is required to make this a possibility. Meanwhile we agree that even as a coalition Respect could be far more effective, proactive and dynamic: we agree with both George and Salma when they underline the need to organise Respect as a coalition in a much more coherent and inclusive way, and to raise its profile.

There are numerous factors behind the present impasse Respect has reached, and George rightly points to some of them:

a) There are serious problems of democratic functioning in Respect, which is a barrier to recruitment. This includes the functioning of the office and the selective implementation of decisions. (There are numerous examples of this, for example: the officers agreed on several occasions

---

CONTINUED FROM PAGE 11

Friday 26 October
Article appears in East London Advertiser re the split in Tower Hamlets.
Respect Appeal against the witch hunt – ie SWP petition – is sent to all Respect members from the Respect national office.

Saturday 27 October
Jerry Hicks resigns from SWP.

Sunday 28 October
Meeting between SWP and *Respect at Crossroads* supporters, agrees formula for amicable separation in principle, and agrees to reconvene on Wednesday 31 October, to finalise details.

Monday 29 October
John Rees appears at Tower Hamlets press conference with 4 councillors who have split from Respect group in Tower Hamlets to form a rival group.
17 members of National Council issue letter to Respect members expressing outrage at Press conference.

Tuesday 30 October
SWP cancel meeting scheduled for following day and any further negotiations. They now say that "the conference must decide".

that the full acronym – respect, socialism, peace, environment, community, trade unionism – should be used on all publications. This failed to happen in most instances. The original proposal for a trade union conference with a big priority towards organising it jointly with the TU left and the CPB was never pursued).

b) There have long been problems with Respect's profile at public events and demonstrations. The Manchester paper has certainly been a positive development in this. We agree with George when he says: "In every area of activity we need to encourage our members to focus on recruitment, fundraising, establishing the profile of our candidates and unashamedly promoting Respect as the critical force in the wider reconstitution of the progressive and socialist movement". The weakness on this is partly because Respect is one of the few organisations on the left which does not have its own paper, even though our meetings, conferences and rallies are seen as venues to sell newspapers from almost every other current on the left.

c) Respect has failed to respond to the failure of the Labour left to mount a challenge to Brown in the leadership election. This issue was discussed (at our instigation) at the last National Council, at which numerous suggestions were made by us, by George and by other NC members – but none were implemented and nothing has happened. The Morning Star/CPB organised a conference to discuss the new situation, as did the RMT; but Respect – which has been the most important left initiative for many years – has done nothing.

The recent Morning Star article by Rob Griffiths, raising the issue of the need for a new party, is an important development. We have to promote a dialogue with such potential allies and build their confidence in what we are doing. We cannot simply say "here is Respect, it is the best thing around (which is certainly true) and you should join it". We have to show them that we are a serious, active, inclusive, campaigning organisation. If Respect is to seriously build itself, it has to convince those coming from the labour and trade union left that there is a democratic space within Respect in which they can function.

Also – partly as a result of Respect's failure to promote itself as a convincing alternative that can win support from trade union leaders – the RMT is considering standing candidates in the GLA elections. We should welcome this development — but do everything we can to reach an agreement with the RMT for a joint slate in these elections.

d) It is difficult to comment on the financial points George makes. There has always been a lack of transparency in financial administration which has made the functioning of the organisation and democratic decision-making very difficult. The NC rarely takes a financial report, and never a detailed one. Yet "off-message" proposals are often met with claims that "there is not the money" while others go through.

There are also issues on which we would go much further than George does in his letter:

1 The first of these is the wider issue of democracy, particularly the accountability of elected representatives – and we welcome what John Rees is now saying about this. Respect members have to be confident that our elected representatives function under the direction of the elected bodies and in line with agreed policy, with differences of opinion managed collectively. Far too often we find out what George is doing – appearing in Big Brother (the most controversial with many of us); not standing for Parliament next time; standing for Parliament next time; standing for the European Parliament, etc – from the media, and not through Respect, and when it is already to late for a collective approach.

The NC has no involvement, that we are aware of, in what George does in Parliament. We need to connect the work in the councils and in Parliament more directly to the leadership bodies. Officers or NC members are unable to take responsibility for what the organisation does in these important areas of work unless they are well informed about it.

2 We need to get rid of the slate system for elections of Respect's leadership at conference and introduce a method which is less alienating to independents. Respect needs to be super-democratic if it is to attract experienced people who are fed up with the Labour Party. Respect structures need to be less vertical with more connection with the branches, which is why we proposed, at the last conference, a delegate-based National Council.

3 On profile, Respect's own regular national publication would give substance and direction to local branches between big events. Set-piece rallies are very good, but how to build Respect effectively when the rally is over, particularly in the weaker areas, is not so clear.

4 Respect has to have a political life separate from its participating organisations. Its leading members have to be in a position to make building Respect a genuine priority in their political work, and prioritise building a collective, inclusive leadership that sets out to draw together the strengths and the talents of all the currents and independent forces that rally to Respect. In our view that means taking on the character of a political party which can collectivise political experience.

5 There is the issue of political profile (policy and programme), which is not mentioned in George's letter.

Respect must have clear socialist politics. This does not mean that we have to mention socialism in every sentence, but Respect has to be within a consistent socialist framework. The current leaflet for the GLA campaign is politically bland and does not mention socialism at all. The same with the London broad sheet published in the Spring. It has no mention of socialism beyond the masthead and no mention of the environment from cover to cover. Almost all of it would be acceptable to a Lib Dem (apart from anti-privatisation) and all of it would be acceptable to the greens. If we are not politically distinct from the greens what is the point?

It would be a big mistake to go into the coming election, facing Gordon Brown, with this type of election material. Any left party wanting to make its mark under these conditions will have to have clear and distinct socialist politics on which to build the campaign.

It will also need strong material on the environment and on climate change if we are to challenge the greens and connect with young people across the country. Respect has strong positions on climate change in its policy document – but the issue has remained marginal in most Respect literature.

The debate on "communalism"

We can have a legitimate debate around new constituencies (sections of the working class) won to Respect – particularly when they are minority communities with which the left has no experience. There may have been over emphasis on particular communities to the detriment of others – that can be discussed. And political concessions may have been made (dropping of an adequate socialist profile for example) in the course

of this that can also be discussed. But this is not "communalism". It is an outrageous charge, which should be withdrawn.

Moreover Respect came out of the anti-war movement, recruited from the anti-war movement, and won its electoral base from the anti-war movement. It was a major breakthrough, unprecedented on the left, into minority communities in East London, Birmingham and Preston in particular. Bringing sections of new radicalising communities into a left-wing organisation was never going to be easy.

We gather there is now much debate around the situation in Birmingham and in particular Tower Hamlets – where apparently there are major problems. It is hard for us to make any judgement on these disputes. None of these problems has been brought in any understandable way into the meetings of the NC. There were a few reports on the work of the councillors, but the battles in Tower Hamlets now being referred to were never raised. No doubt there are problems and conflicts: but such problems are probably inevitable when such breakthroughs are made by the left into new sections of the working class – whether minority communities or not.

The question is not whether there have been and will be political problems and disagreements: the question is whether political steps were taken to discuss these problems openly and bring about a common political development.

Was there discussion on the issues involved? Has Respect developed any systematic political education on a more general basis? The answer, unfortunately, is no.

Practical steps

The organisation has been going backwards and now faces a crisis. No change is not a viable option.

The conference in November needs to build a new and broader unity in the leadership bodies and make the necessary changes which can take the organisation forward and build it as a broad, active, high-profile, campaigning party to the left of New Labour, which in our view should also run an active publicity machine and a high profile campaigning publication. This would present a strong and credible appeal to the left in the trade unions, the demoralised left in the Labour Party, and to the Morning Star/CPB. Any other answer threatens to undermine all of the gains that have been made so far, and all of the good work that has been done so far at national and local level to build Respect.

CHALLENGES FOR RESPECT

by Councillor Salma Yaqoob – National Vice Chair

George's document accurately outlines the two biggest challenges and responsibilities we face today: "to build Respect directly and to place it at the centre of a progressive realignment". In order for Respect to rise to these challenges there are some foundation stones that must be in place.

Firstly, if Respect aspires to be a coalition of individuals and organisations from quite divergent political backgrounds, but united against imperialism and neo-liberalism, it is imperative that the internal political culture inside Respect is one that is at ease with difference and pluralism and not threatened by it.

Secondly, Respect has to proactively seek to embrace the broadest currents of progressive opinion if it is to fulfil the aspirations behind its launch.

The need for Respect

The need for a party to the left of Labour is more urgent than ever. This is confirmed for me on the second Tuesday of every month, when I attend the meeting of Birmingham city councillors. It is indicative of the sorry state of affairs of the Labour Party that they are regularly outflanked to the left by the Tories.

Under New Labour, wealth inequality and privatisation have increased dramatically. Gordon Brown calls on public-sector workers to accept a cut in their real level of pay, while 1% of the population owns one-third of all personal wealth in this country. Where the Tories only managed to sign 100 PFI deals with big business, Brown has delivered more than 600 wasteful and privatising schemes.

Meanwhile, Liberty argues that the government is 'laying the infrastructure of Orwell's Big Brother state' and we see the ever-increasing beat of US war drums against Iran.

Despite the significant obstacles the first past the post system poses for smaller parties, I remain convinced and committed to the future of this project.

The broad constituency in favour of peace, equality and social justice is growing. On many issues it is even a majority in society. Millions of people are against war, against privatising and running down the welfare state, against racism, and for greater equality. There is an opportunity to be a voice for these millions, and to offer an electoral alternative to the parties of war and injustice.

Facing realities

Despite the growing number of people who oppose imperialism and neo-liberalism, the balance remains in favour of the parties of war, privatisation and racism.

Tony Blair won the 2005 election in the face of mass protests against the war. The growth of the BNP across the country far exceeds our own modest successes. Yes, Labour will lose seats at the next election. But the vast majority of them will be lost to parties to their right.

Respect therefore faces a situation where there is widespread and growing sympathy for the type of ideas we espouse, but where the parties of the right are increasing their stranglehold on electoral politics.

In a situation where our opponents remain far stronger than us, it is essential that we seek to operate in the most consensual and pluralistic manner possible, open to cooperation with all those, regardless of party, who share our commitment to peace, equality and justice.

This will be impossible if Respect is perceived as the property of a single organisation. To build a coalition of like-minded individuals and organisations we must go the extra mile in our efforts to include different voices and experiences. We have to consciously and proactively demonstrate to all those outside Respect that they have a place in our coalition, and that by joining us they are signing up to a genuine coalition in which no single component of it is in a position to impose its views.

If our coalition is currently insuffici-ently broad, it is all the more important that we act, and are seen to act, in such a way as to reflect the coalition we want to be.

The challenge for Respect is to be able to work with, and be a voice for, this growing broad progressive constituency. This constituency includes people who remain tied to Labour or other parties such as the Greens. We have to work patiently to build up our vote at a local level. But we also have to be part (and almost certainly a minority part) of a much wider network of alliances.

George has pointed to the urgency of initiatives in the aftermath of Blair's resignation to capitalise on the space for a discussion on left realignment. This discussion is also taking place outside Respect. For example the recent Morning Star conference and articles. And, in a different way, they are taking place in and around the Labour Party.

We have not been bold enough in taking initiatives to further this potential dialogue.

Respect needs a more democratic and inclusive internal political culture

Having taken the first steps towards bringing together a new party to the left of Labour we need to encourage an internal culture that is far more inclusive and participative.

If it is not seen that we operate in a genuinely collaborative manner, if we cannot manage our differences in a non-factional manner, we have no hope of being the pole of attraction to those disaffected with Labour and looking for an alternative. George's proposals about strengthening the role of the national office with a new national organiser to work alongside the national secretary and a revamped officers committee are changes that need to be introduced. In the run up to conference we should also conduct a thorough examination of our current practice.

Why is it that Respect has such an uneven profile – not just across the country, but also even within areas where we have made headway like London and Birmingham? How do we make ourselves more attractive to those disaffected with the current political system but nervous about Respect?

How can we improve our public events? How do we strengthen the political depth of our activists and better shape the political culture within the organisation? Is the slate system the most democratic method of electing delegates to our national bodies? Is it the case that we convey the impression that Respect is dominated by a single organisation? If so, what can we do about it?

Many members have expressed dismay that, while their organisation is in the midst of this debate, no reference to it is made on our website and they have to scour the net to glean a greater understanding as to what the debate is actually about. There should be space on our national website for internal discussion and the posting of internal documents.

Damaging allegations

Unfortunately, the manner in which this current debate is being conducted is a bad advertisement.

Misrepresentation of views is perhaps a feature of these kinds of rows, but that does not make them any more excusable. It is, unfortunately, necessary to deal with two rather unpleasant allegations that have been introduced into this debate.

Firstly, it is not the case that I oppose the diversity of Respect candidates in favour of Muslim men, as claimed by the SWP.

As one of the few Muslim women in a prominent political position, I am more aware than most of the obstacles that are in our way, and the importance of bringing more woman (in particular) into leading political positions.

In Birmingham, four out of five candidates in the 2006 local elections were women. But in 2007, only one woman sought a nomination. All the other nominations were from Asian male candidates. In the only contested election the one woman prospective candidate was defeated but I wrote to Socialist Worker (10 February) specifically urging SWP members to come forward as candidates for any of the other 33 wards that we could have contested. No other nominations were made, leaving us with 7 male candidates.

Even more upsetting have been accusations around "communalist politics" in Birmingham as reflected in the SWP Party Notes of 7 March 2007.

The allegation of communalism has been thrown at Respect from our enemies, and it is disturbing to see echoes of it inside Respect. Only those ignorant of my record, or hostile to my work, could make such a charge.

The fault line of 'communalist politics' in Birmingham has most recently been between African-Caribbean and Asian communities, who often feel in competition with each other over council funding. These tensions tragically ignited in Lozells where two young people lost their lives. There is no political figure in Birmingham more closely associated with trying to address these tensions than myself.

That is why I initiated the women and children's Peace March in the aftermath of the Lozells riots, which received very high local news coverage. That is why Respect supporters took great risks, behind the scenes, to ensure there was no retaliation from Pakistani gangs in the aftermath of the desecration of Muslim graves in Handsworth cemetery. When I spoke from the platform of the recent Jesse Jackson rally to a 600 strong (and overwhelmingly African-Caribbean) audience, I used my time to call for black and Asian unity. It is not accidental that I was the only politician to speak at the recent march in Lozells against Gangs and Guns organised by the Council of Black led Churches.

Furthermore, both in my newsletters and within the council chamber I have specifically championed the issue of poor educational attainment of white working class boys from disadvantaged backgrounds.

If I wanted to pander to conservative pressure inside the Muslim community, appearing on Question Time and opposing the imposition of Islamic dress on women, opposing the criminalisation of women in the sex industry, or opposing homophobia in the local media, would not exactly be the best way to go about it!

It is hard to think of a more damaging allegation than that of communalism. It can only sour relations between us and give ammunition to our enemies.

False divisions

Differences have to be discussed with restraint, and communication and dialogue is the key. Unfortunately, since I disagreed with John Rees over an issue of tactics in July 2005, I don't think I have received more than 2 phone calls from him. Personal feelings are not the issue. The National Secretary should be able to maintain working relationships and act as a link to all parts of Respect. He should consult widely to learn from everyone's experience.

It is disingenuous also to make references to my inability to attend National Officers meetings when no effort was made to act on my request to hold meetings on web cam to facilitate those of us who don't live in London and have childcare and family commitments. A leadership striving to be as inclusive as possible would be imaginative and proactive about encouraging participation, especially of those with childcare and family responsibilities.

It is also disingenuous to misrepresent the issues as being at heart about whether John Rees should or should not resign. Neither George nor myself have called for John Rees's resignation. In our meeting I commented to John that had I been in his shoes I would have stepped down, but I also made it explicit that I was not making this a formal demand in any way, and was advocating only those demands outlined in George's document. For the SWP to report this as a formal call for his resignation is a deliberate distortion, designed perhaps to distract from the real issues raised.

What I find most insidious about these allegations is not only that they are false, but that they have been deliberately circulated to foster divisions and exacerbate differences within Respect.

If the SWP leadership had issues of concerns about the political direction in Birmingham, particularly if they felt something as serious as a 'pandering to communalism' was taking place, the very least I would expect is that these concerns would be communicated directly to myself or raised openly inside Respect. Neither has happened.

Instead, it appears these claims, and others, are designed entirely to marshall SWP members with pseudo ideological cover in what is really a drive for control. Overall it has hindered, not helped, Respect and no doubt has been counter productive for the SWP itself. The interests of one factional bloc have been put above the broader interests of Respect itself. This method has caused confusion and poisoned relations between people who otherwise had got on well up to that point.

This highlights an important issue of principle for Respect if we are to be seen as a genuine coalition and not a front for one component part – whether that is the SWP today or a "independents' bloc' tomorrow. We have to build into the culture, and maybe also the constitution of Respect, safeguards that compel us to work in a collaborative and not a competitive manner. In our internal dealings we have to enact the values of openness, transparency, pluralism and democracy that we espouse in broader society. In this way there will be consistency between our goals and our process, which will only strengthen us. It involves short-term compromise for long-term gain.

My experience with ordinary SWP members has overwhelmingly been a positive one. They are committed, sincere and hard working activists. I value their contribution to Respect and other campaigns. I do not want to see the SWP outside Respect, and I continue to hope that they will play an important role in building Respect. I have been saddened by the unnecessary deterioration in relations.

Conflating legitimate criticisms of the National Secretary with allegations of plots to 'subordinate' socialist elements in Respect, also only compounds our problems.

The notion that 'the socialist left' is in danger of being subordinated inside Respect can only be read as patronising. The inference is that, without a guiding hand, the rest of us (especially Muslims) would quickly gallop to the right and pander to all manner of prejudices. I do not accept that the SWP is the sole guarantor of the progressive values around which we have united.

While the well from which I draw my commitment to social justice may be a different one, it is every bit as deep. It was out of this very commitment to genuine progressive values that I helped initiate Respect.

Respect needs to build on its electoral strengths. On a national scale, our electoral successes are modest. But, in particular areas, we have really made an impact.

In East London, Birmingham and Preston we have developed a real base, with much of our support coming from Muslims. This is a strength, which we should celebrate. Opposition to the war on Iraq ran deepest among Muslims. Pakistani and Bangladeshi communities, in particular, are among the most disadvantaged in our society. The constant attacks on the views and way of life of Muslims have produced deep anger. All of these factors serve to highlight the inadequacy of political representation at a local level, and the very limited representation for Muslim communities at a national level.

The fact that Respect has won a serious base in some Muslim communities is a tremendous achievement for all of us. For the first time, a part of the genuine left has sunk deep roots in some of the most disadvantaged communities in the country. In a period where racism is on the rise, and multiculturalism is under attack, the importance of this is hard to overestimate.

We have been much weaker in areas where this combination of factors is not as strong. But this is not, as has been unhelpfully suggested by the SWP, evidence of a lack of commitment to 'widen and diversify Respect's working class support'.

George's letter specifically highlighted the contributions of Michael Lavalette in Preston, Jerry Hicks in Bristol and Maxine Blower in Sheffield – all white, socialist candidates. No one in Respect thinks that we are, or should be, a 'Muslim party'. On the contrary, what we have tried to achieve is the coming together of people from very different traditions and backgrounds by stressing the common ground between us. This vision, which was at the heart of the discussions which led to the formation of Respect, remains as strong today as it was then.

There are whole swathes of white working class areas that feel abandoned. We need an honest discussion inside Respect about what we have committed to these areas, apart from rhetoric.

It is not true, either, that this argument is about whether

Respect should withdraw "into the electoral common sense that only particular 'community leaders' can win in certain areas".

But the reality is that the strongest candidates will invariably be those who are the most locally rooted. This is electoral common sense. The Respect brand is simply not strong enough that we can parachute candidates into areas where they have no local roots and hope to do well. Wherever this method has been applied the outcome has been poor and damaging to us.

Sustained local community activity is the key to ensuring strong local candidates and every potential Respect candidate should aim to be a 'community leader' if they are serious about trying to win. Part of our role is to be able to bring the respected and rooted local activist (or 'community leader') into the wider progressive alliance that we have created, and for us all to be strengthened by this common ground.

We need an open and frank discussion about the state of many Respect branches.

Too often we just do not undertake the hard slog of embedding ourselves in local communities by consistently addressing their local issues and concerns.

Building coaches for anti-war demos, or working in your trade union, is important. If you want to be elected as a councillor the electorate will also want to see the same passion and commitment about the local issues that are impacting on their lives.

Too often our organising skills are not focused enough on consistent local campaigns, advice surgeries and following-up on casework. Similarly attending resident associations or neighbourhood forums is rarely a priority, although these are often the arenas where local people gather to express their concerns.

We need to combine in our local work both a commitment to campaigning around the big political issues and addressing ways these link to specific local issues that impact on people's day-to-day lives.

We need to work consciously and patiently to consolidate and extend our vote in our existing strongholds. And, where we are weaker, we need to begin to act as if we were already local councillors. The crisis of political representation extends right down to ward level. We have to be willing and able to offer an alternative now.

Conclusion

There are many people outside Respect who should be in Respect. By accepting George's proposals we have an opportunity to strengthen a culture of participation and pluralism that clearly signals our willingness to be a genuine coalition. We have an opportunity to show, in practice, that we are a home for those seeking an alternative to the right-wing consensus.

There are many more people outside Respect, who share many

of our principles but who, for a variety of reasons and party loyalties, may not join us at the moment. Our willingness to be open and flexible in co-operating and sharing ideas and experiences is vital for the future of us all.

My vision for Respect is of a coalition which acts to support all those who share a commitment to peace, equality and justice. In building Respect we have to act in a way that strengthens this broad progressive constituency and does not divide it.

A NEW CRISIS OR A NEW OPPORTUNITY?

Report on the Respect NC meetings: Alan Thornett

Just when the need for a party like Respect is clearer than ever, with the arrival of Brown and the snuffing out of the last vestiges of democracy in the Labour Party, Respect has been passing through the biggest crisis in its three-and-a-half year history.

After a series of statements and resolutions and two National Council meetings, the jury is out on whether enough has been done to re-launch Respect on a broader and more inclusive basis. It is also out on whether the political will exists in the SWP leadership to positively implement the decisions adopted which could take the organisation forward.

The crisis came to a head around two critical meetings of the Respect National Council on September 22, which failed to complete its agenda, and another the following week on September 29 to complete the business.

At the centre of the crisis was a serious rift between some of Respect's major components: the SWP on the one hand and George Galloway, Salma Yaqoob, and some of the East London councillors on the other. It was described by George Galloway as a breakdown of trust, and it clearly was and is.

These events were triggered by a letter from George Galloway to the NC which raised a number of legitimate issues. It argued that Respect has not fulfilled its potential in terms of either votes or membership, and that in some areas Respect is effectively moribund. It implicitly criticised the method used by the SWP regarding decision-making and priorities. It also implicitly challenged the SWP approach to Respect, which is to treat it as an electoral united front (of a special kind).

There did not have to be a crisis over such criticisms, however, a number of which some of us have been raising for a long time. The SWP leadership grossly over-reacted – seeing the letter as an attack on the SWP itself, and John Rees in particular, and responding in that vein. A positive response and an undertaking to make some changes (even some concessions) and tackle some of the issues Galloway was raising could have created a very different situation.

By the time of the September 22 NC therefore, instead of compromise, the debate was ratcheted up. In internal meetings of the SWP (the contents of which leaked into the public domain) inflammatory charges of communalism had been levelled at George Galloway, Salma Yaqoob and some of the East London councillors. The clash was presented as a left versus right issue, or the socialists versus the communalists. These accusations were then repeated in the course of the National Committee meeting. It was bound to raise the heat whether or not it was designed to do so.

There was heavy criticism of Tower Hamlets group – which reflects Respect's unique breakthrough into the Muslim community by the predominantly white left. It is not surprising that there are problems following such a breakthrough, but these problems have never been brought to the NC for collective discussion. The question is not whether there have been political problems and disagreements. The question is whether political steps were taken to discuss these problems and bring about a common political development.

John Lister and I had submitted a discussion paper to the NC taking up these issues and other aspects of the debate as had Salma Yaqoob – who made a very powerful case against the communalism allegation.

In the debate on all this on the 22nd, speaker after speaker from the SWP (of their 19 members on the NC) attacked George Galloway, in particular, around these issues. The result was a blow-up in which George Galloway announced that he would not be a candidate in the upcoming election and came close to walking out.

Fortunately he did not walk out, and fortunately he has reversed his decision and is putting himself forward in Poplar and Canning Town.

I have been amongst the harshest critics of George Galloway, particularly over the issue of accountability. But the notion that Respect could fight a successful election campaign in six weeks' time (or six months' time), or successfully approach other sections of the left and the trade unions in order to expand outwards after a fractious split with George Galloway, was an illusion. We could have said goodbye to a new left party for a long time.

The meeting moved on to discuss the practical proposals in George Galloway's letter, which he moved in summary form. His most controversial proposal, as far as the SWP was concerned, was for a new post of national organiser to function alongside the national secretary (aimed at broadening Respect out at the top).

The SWP, however, saw this as a direct challenge to the authority of John Rees, and therefore to the vertical control which is implicit in both the method of the SWP and its model for Respect as one a number of united fronts in which they work. It was this which made a simple proposal emerge as a pivotal issue.

The argument the SWP used was that any elected position took precedent over any appointed one. This arose because the new post would need to be appointed if it was to be open to the whole membership rather than just the NC. But why would an elected post take precedent? Providing they were both responsible to the same elected committees which could regulate their work, there was no need for one to be the line manager of the other. There is nothing in Respect's constitution which requires such a thing. And when the issue was to re-establish trust it made no sense to insist on such an arrangement.

George Galloway's proposals were therefore accepted with the proviso that the apparently vexed issue of the authority/ constitutionality of a national organiser alongside the national secretary, would be discussed by a working group comprising Ger Francis, Lindsey German, Linda Smith and myself, in an attempt to find solution.

We met but failed to agree. I could agree with everything Lindsey German wrote with the exception of the last three words "and individual officers". These words reversed the proposal (that both officers are responsible to the EC) and put the national secretary back in charge. I discussed it with her prior to the 29th (we met over another issue) but to no avail.

The first item on the agenda on the 29th was Respect's approach to the looming general election. It was a good discussion. It is clearly crucial that the left is able to mount a credible challenge to new Labour under Brown in a snap poll. And that means Respect, because no other left grouping has the ability to ripple the surface of the water.

Respect has at least the possibility of winning in three constituencies in such an election.

Two of these are in East London: Bethnal Green and Bow – currently George Galloway's constituency – and Poplar and Canning Town, where Respect recently won the Shadwell local by-election and which is the constituency of Government Minister Jim Fitzpatrick. The other is Birmingham Sparkbrook and Small Heath, where Salma Yaqoob came a close second in 2005.

It is a mammoth task, of course. But just being a serious challenger in these seats informs the shape of Respect's election campaign. It means that Respect will stand in a limited number of seats chosen (probably less than the 25 seats Respect stood in 2005) so that support can be given to the constituencies with the best chance of success whilst mounting a challenge in other selected areas.

The meeting voted unanimously to urge George Galloway, who had not yet made a decision, to put himself forward for one of the East London seats. He said he would seriously reconsider in light of the decision, and many other such requests he had had. A letter was handed to him by Jerry Hicks to this effect from Bristol Respect.

The meeting then returned to the issue of the national organiser. The old debate began to re-run but it was difficult to sustain. When I said that I could accept all Lindsey German was proposing other than the last three words, she said she had no problem in deleting them. John Rees said the same, and that was it. The two would work side by side and report to the elected committees. We had an agreement which we could have had a week earlier.

George Galloway's other proposal for a new, broader, and more inclusive executive committee is also very important. The narrow nature of the existing committee led myself and John Lister to decline nomination to it after last year's conference. It was too narrow to function effectively, and was not in reality an authoritative decision making body. Changing this and broadening the committee out will be the task of the incoming NC after the November conference. Also the overpowering size of the SWP delegations on the committees has to come to an end.

Resolutions for conference

The next item on the agenda was NC resolutions to Respect conference. Here the meeting unanimously adopted a resolution I moved, which incorporated the resolution tabled by myself and John Lister at the previous meeting, and the resolution adopted at that meeting moved by George Galloway. This combined resolution was seconded by John Rees who had proposed some amendments to it prior to the meeting.

It was crucial that this went through. The resolution offers a new way forward for Respect both in terms of tasks and priorities and in opening up Respect to the broader movement. In fact, if fully implemented it could re-launch Respect on a more open and attractive basis.

Central to the resolution is the need to engage others on the left such as the RMT, the CPB, Bob Wareing and John McDonnell, who are currently discussing the issue of labour representation in the light of the rise of Brown.

The resolution urges that: "These discussions to be on the basis of no organisational preconditions as far as Respect is concerned, with the aim of initiating a process towards a wider regroupment of left forces." This could hardly be more urgent, given the escalating debate around this issue.

The resolution proposes approaching these organisations and individuals with a view to jointly organising a conference with them on the crisis of representation and the way forward. This should be held as soon as practically possible and built on the broadest possible basis.

The resolution also proposes a number of other measures designed to build Respect more effectively, recruit new members and reinvigorate the branches:

... On public profile: "To build a much higher public profile for Respect. To have an effective means of getting our ideas across through broad sheets and leaflets, and an improved, revitalised website and improved media management with a well resourced press officer. We agree in principle to produce a newspaper or a magazine. This should be discussed by a working party and brought back to the NC for implementation in the New Year".

... To end the slate system of election at Respect conference, which has been contentious with individual activists, from the upcoming conference in 2007, and the introduction of a form of STV, to be agreed.

... To introduce a partly delegate-based National Council with delegates from the branches – from the 2008 conference

... To improve communications and accountability and overhaul the organisation of the national office.

On electoral policy, the resolution stresses the need to ensure that Respect has clear working class politics in the campaign. "This means that the ethos of Respect as expressed in its acronym Respect, Equality, Socialism, Peace, Environment, Community, Trade Unionism, has to be the framework of its work, its activities and its policies. Any left party wanting to make its mark under the current conditions will have to have clear and distinct and radical politics on which to build an election campaign".

It resolves to ensure that Respect plays an integral part in the struggle of the trade unions against the Brown wage freeze and the attack on trade union rights, and against privatisation and deregulation and to continue to support the activities and campaigns of the StWC both in terms of opposition to the war and

the defence of civil liberties and human rights.

It also stresses the need to ensure that: "Respect gives a high profile to material on the environment and climate change in its election and general material. To become more involved in the climate change campaign and the climate camps and their activities. Support the climate change trade union conference". This is not only necessary in its own right, given the huge urgency of the issue, but essential if Respect is going to challenge the Greens and attract young people to its campaign.

These proposals do offer a way forward at a time of great potential opportunity. Ultimately, however, it is in the hands of the SWP. According to the various reports of the SWP party council, the day after the NC business as usual was apparently the order of the day. If this was the case the signs are not good.

To maximise the impact of Respect in today's conditions, the culture of the organisation has to change and this has to go right down to the branches. The opportunities to build a broad-based left alternative have never been greater; but if the left manages to miss it, it could be a long time before it comes around again.

WHAT IS COMMUNALISM?

Andy Newman

The accusations that Respect relies upon a communalist appeal towards Muslim voters were originally mainly heard from out-and-out opponents of the Respect project.

It has been entirely to the credit of the SWP that they succeeded in developing a strong relationship with Muslim activists and intellectuals during the lead up to the Iraq war, and that the Stop the War Coalition involved substantial numbers of Muslims as well as black and other ethnic minorities.

This fed into the electoral success of Respect within Muslim communities. As Murray Smith argued in *The European elections and the anti-capitalist left*:

"The impact that Respect has had among Muslim and immigrant communities represents a huge step forward. There is nothing to disagree with in what Alex Callinicos says there. The question of '(winning) the support of a working class that in the inner cities at least, is increasingly diverse in its colours, national origins, and religious beliefs' is one that confronts socialists not just in Britain but in just about every country of Europe. In most of them a great deal remains to be done. In France the gulf between the left and immigrant communities is considerable, a situation not helped by prevailing attitudes among many on the left to the affirmation of minority identities, especially when they are expressed through religion. There are historical reasons which explain but do not excuse the attitudes of a large part of the French left towards Islam and religion in general. It is perhaps not too much to hope that the success of Respect among Muslims in Britain might encourage some on the French left to rethink their attitudes."

As I argued at the launch of Respect:

"There has been success in involving 'ethnic community' activists and intellectuals – most prominently from a Muslim background, but also involving many in Turkish and Kurdish organisations'. As Will McMahon reports from a Respect meeting in North London: 'There was clearly a new layer of people who had been drawn to the meeting by the Respect campaign. A group of Kurdish and Turkish supporters were joined by people from a local mosque and the Afro-Caribbean community. These gains were also seen on the battle bus, where the megaphone was delivering messages in Kurdish, Turkish and Gujurati. Small but significant gains have been made in this regard over the course of the campaign. New forces are involved and further progress is possible.' This is one area where Respect – and the SWP – can be rightly proud."

It was therefore surprising to read SWP National Secretary Martin Smith in the SWP's internal mailing, SWP Party Notes, sent out on 5th March 2007, saying that in "Birmingham … serious elements of Respect are pulled by communalist forces".

Communalism is a term that has a clear meaning in the context of the politics of the Indian sub-continent and, as Achin Vanaik has argued, has "a negative connotation of bigotry, divisiveness and parochialism", and it "helps to harden the divisions between different religious communities and increase tensions between them". The question relates to binding politics to particular religious identities, in order to promote one's own religious community at the expense of other communities.

It is therefore very important to note Salma Yaqoob's account of Respect's role in Birmingham:

"The fault line of 'communalist politics' in Birmingham has most recently been between African-Caribbean and Asian communities who often feel in competition with each other over council funding. There is no political figure in Birmingham more closely associated with trying to address these tensions than myself. That is why I initiated the women and children's Peace March in the aftermath of the Lozells riots which cost the lives of two young black

men. Respect supporters took great risks, behind the scenes, to ensure there was no retaliation from Pakistani gangs in the aftermath of the desecration of Muslim graves. When I spoke from the platform of the recent Jesse Jackson rally to a 600 strong (and overwhelmingly African-Caribbean) audience, I used my time to call for black and Asian unity. Furthermore, both in my newsletters and within the council chamber, I have specifically championed the issue of poor educational attainment of white working class boys from disadvantaged backgrounds."

So quite the opposite of communal-ism as the term is commonly understood, Salma Yaqoob and Birmingham Respect have been undermining communalism.

As Salma also says: "The accusation of 'communalism' is also used by some as code for Respect's elected representatives who are Muslim, and the supposed manner in which they pander to reactionary views supposedly more prevalent among Muslims. This is equally dangerous in the way that it 'racialises' debates that run throughout every section of society. The chauvinist identification of Muslims as a threat to 'our' values undermines the very significant advances we have made on spreading a progressive and unifying message."

Here is an abridged extract from Achin Vanaik's article *Reflections on Communalism and Nationalism in India* from

New Left Review I/196, November-December 1992

You can read a longer extract here. Those bandying about the term communalism should think hard about what the term means, and whose company they are keeping by using it.

Communalism

The term 'communalism' was first used by British colonialists to describe the situation of colonies like India and Malaysia, where religious minorities existed alongside a religious majority. The colonial use of the term gave it a negative connotation of bigotry, divisiveness and parochialism, thus helping to justify the colonial civilizing mission. It was also a way of understanding Indian history as colonialists saw and lived it. It apparently corresponded to the pattern of colonial expansion – defeat of the Mughal Empire, of Hindu princely kingdoms, of Ranjit Singh's Sikh empire. Indian nationalists adopted the term, accepted its negative significations, but saw it as a colonial, post-British phenomenon rather than a pre-colonial circumstance that the British inherited.

My own provisional and tentative definition of communalism in a religiously plural society is as follows: it is a process involving competitive de-secularisation (a competitive striving to extend the reach and power of religions), which – along with non-religious factors – helps to harden the divisions between different religious communities and increase tensions between them. Here greater importance is granted to religious forces, religious identity, religious competition, religious ideologies and to religious input into popular, folk and elite cultures. The development of a strong collective religious identity among Hindus, Sikhs, Muslims and Christians is not a sufficient condition for the growth of communalism, but it is seen as a necessary one. Moreover, non-religious factors are not excluded as important causal factors. Indeed, the non-religious is often misperceived in religious terms.

Communal Politics

A 'materialist' analysis of the sources of communalism in the colonial and post-colonial period would reveal the role of the colonial state in deliberately exacerbating the communal divide. Competition for jobs created tensions between Hindu and Muslim urban middle classes and elites. In post-Independence India, attention would no doubt be focused on the socio-economic changes that have taken place in many northern Indian towns possessing a sizeable Muslim population, as a result of Gulf remittances, the growing export demand for handicrafts and artisanal products, and other expressions of uneven development. These have been among the socio-economic changes that have clearly disturbed traditional patterns of dependence between Hindu traders and Muslim artisans. Similarly, Green Revolution effects in Punjab are not without communal resonance for the Sikh kulak and Hindu trader. Then again, there is the upward economic and political mobility of the agrarian bourgeoisie, of the upper echelons of the intermediate castes, and this has had its social and emotional reflection in a greater striving towards association with a broader Hindu identity. There is nothing wrong with such explanations. They are an important part of the story, but only a part.

There is also a second question: why the success of the communal appeal? Here it becomes impossible to maintain any artificial separation between 'true' or 'folk' religion on the one hand and communalism on the other. For what unites 'folk' and 'elite' religion, its 'authentic' and 'inauthentic' forms, is something intrinsic to the nature of all the main world religions—Judaism, Islam, Christianity, Buddhism and Hinduism. We are here on the socio-psychological terrain of identity, of the relationship (never static) between religious belief and the socio-psychic need to affix one's sense of self, or more correctly one's senses of selves. The communal appeal thus derives much of its formidable character not just from the resources of power accumulated by the one making the appeal, but also from the importance of religious identity in the psychic health of the receiver. This is not to invest it with incontestable powers. The importance of religious identity is itself a historical and social variable.

In the later modernizing societies of the post-colonial countries, where the state played an important role in carrying out something of a forced industrialization, there is all the more reason to expect sharper disparities between the modernising-secularising pretensions of the state and the slower-changing realities of civil societies. In India, a non-denominational state with substantially secularised laws, resting on a basically secular Constitution, coexists with a civil society where religious influence is pervasive. It is a situation that gives rise to profound tension.

OUT TOWARDS THE OPEN SEA

The following document was written by Nick Wrack as a contribution to the SWP's Pre-conference Internal Bulletin. He was recently expelled from the SWP. Nick is a former national Chairperson of Respect.

The decision to turn the Party outwards towards working with other radical left forces in society, implemented through the various forms of united front work over the past few years, was correct. Such a turn inevitably brings with it new problems as the party collectively, and comrades individually, are forced to confront new situations and to consider different ways of working.

Respect is the most significant and the most important arena for this turn in our work. It arises out of our correct assessment that there is a significant space to the left of Labour, which can be filled by a radical working-class force in which revolutionaries can work with others to build a serious electoral alternative to New Labour. Whatever may be said about the strength and length of the Brown bounce, it cannot fundamentally alter this assessment.

Unfortunately, the theoretical arguments that we have put forward to explain our work in Respect have not been fully worked through; and consequently not all of the necessary conclusions about what Respect is and how we should relate to it, have been properly drawn. This is partly because we have not systematically and regularly discussed these issues as a party. As a result of this absence of dialogue we fail to draw all the correct strategic and tactical conclusions about our work within Respect.

Respect is not a classical united front. Nor is it helpful to describe it as a united front of a special kind, unless the 'special kind' is more clearly explained. Without further explanation or clarification it can lead to errors in our work, particularly the periodic switching on and off of Respect work, which undermine the possibilities for developing Respect.

Respect is a broad political organis-ationthatcontestselections. It puts forward a comprehensive politicalprogramme. It is not a union of forces for a temporary fight on a single or several limited demands but a permanent formation around a wide-ranging political manifesto. Whether it is described as a party or a coalition is immaterial. It stands in elections. It has a manifesto. It has branches. It has an MP and councillors. To the wider world and to most people who join it, it is a party. Those who join it see it as their party. They want to build it, make it more successful.

To achieve this means patient, persistent and consistent work at a local level to create, maintain and develop active Respect branches. Without branches that relate to the local working class communities, successful election campaigns are almost impossible. This means that we have to put into practice our claim that "Respect is not just an electoral organisation". Because unless we act to build Respect on a regular basis across the country, rooted in every locality, we will never be able to have successful election campaigns. This is the lesson of Southall. There is a grave danger that we will suffer in the GLA elections in May 2008 as a consequence of our failure to implement this approach.

Overarching strategic objective

The reason for our failure to approach Respect in this way is primarily that we do not see Respect as the overarching strategic objective for the party in this period. Firstly, we treat it as a united front that can be turned on for elections and then forgotten about for the rest of the time. Secondly, although we carry out many united front operations, we do not link them all back to Respect. We should constantly be trying to see how we can relate our work in DCH, StWC, UAF and our various industrial interventions to the question of building and recruiting to Respect. There is insufficient strategic thinking about how the work can dovetail towards building Respect. This reinforces the weakness of Respect at local and national level. Respect is seen as just another area of united front work, on a par with the others. It is not. It has to be much more

than that. It has to be the most important area of work into which all other areas of work are brought together.

This does not at all mean liquidating the party. On the contrary, it means that the party will carry out work in a broader political milieu, comprising trade unionists, anti-war activists, environmentalists, radicals from Muslim communities, etc. Our political ideas will find fertile ground here. Our task then is to explain patiently the ideas of revolutionary socialism whilst building Respect as an active, campaigning organisation with real purchase in the local and national working class.

When we sell the paper or intervene at work, we do so openly as members of the party. But often we do not also identify as being members of Respect. And when we do Respect work it is often not clearly understood how this contributes to the building of the party. Many comrades do not see Respect work as being an opportunity to raise our wider politics, but as an electoralist, reformist operation: foot-soldiers for others. It is not surprising that many comrades have rebelled against Respect work, as they see it as a watering-down of their revolutionary activity. We need much more discussion about how we intervene in Respect as revolutionaries without creating unnecessary divisions with others involved.

This also raises questions about how we relate to others in

Respect from different traditions and backgrounds. We should be immensely proud of the work we have carried out within Muslim communities. No other political force has been capable of this. We have correctly argued against those who have criticised us for it. We must not succumb to those criticisms now. Our approach within Respect should be informed by the need to broaden the forces involved. Every new member or group that gets involved should be welcomed and encouraged.

New forces will bring with them their own ideas, habits and methods of work. Inevitably this will mean that discussions and disagreements will arise. Sometimes these disagreements may be sharp, but we should not make them so unnecessarily. Nor should we shy away from raising problems and involving all parts of Respect in a discussion to resolve them. So, for example, if there are issues about sexism or homophobia then they should be tackled at the time, not left for months and then raised as a way to beat those who disagree with us. Any formation that manages to involve people from beyond the (very small) traditional left will inevitably have to confront these problems. Our motto should be "to explain patiently". That can only help to raise the understanding of all.

Unfortunately, in the recent crisis, charges of sexism and homophobia have been raised in such a way as to brand a whole community or a section of it, rather than as the backwardness of this or that individual. Even worse has been the charge that we are faced with "communalism". This is an inflammatory charge designed to polarise the debate and can do nothing to resolve disagreements about candidate selection. Anyone who took the time to discuss with the subjects of the accusations would very quickly have to conclude that the term is not appropriate.

It is inevitable, given the electoral successes of Respect, that we will attract people with opportunist inclinations. This is not so shocking. We just need to deal with it. With all things we need most of all a sense of proportion and a sense of perspective. With the launching of Respect we took to the open sea. We need to hold our nerve and carry on, not retreat to the calm of the shore at the first sight of inclement weather. We also need a deft hand at the tiller.

The response from the CC to George Galloway's' letter, however, has shown anything but a sense of proportion or a sense of perspective. If we accept that Respect is critically important and needs to continue, then that has to inform our response to any difficulty or conflict within Respect. Our approach, as the dominant organised force, has to be such that temperatures are reduced, not raised. This is sometimes difficult but necessary.

Firstly, there has been a completely exaggerated description of problems in Tower Hamlets and Birmingham. Secondly, there has been a disproportionate response to these problems and to George Galloway's document. Instead of engaging with the points Galloway raised, the CC responded by taking the party to a war footing, stating that Galloway had declared war on the SWP, that this was a battle of left against right, of the socialists against communalism, and so on. This was to blow the criticisms raised by Galloway so much out of proportion as to engulf the whole of Respect in a crisis that could have been avoided. Lots of comrades involved in small weak Respect branches who look around the country at the absence of Respect branches elsewhere, will relate to much of what Galloway said. We should have engaged with his letter, disagreeing where necessary. But to present it as an attack on the work with trade unions and gay rights was a serious disservice to the party.

There are real problems at the heart of Respect. Personal and political relations have broken down between the leadership of the party and other prominent members, Salma Yaqoob and George Galloway. We need to rectify this. We cannot take the view that it does not matter if Galloway walks away or if Salma goes. They are both vital assets for Respect. They reach an audience and have a constituency way beyond what we could reach on our own. The great strength of Respect is that it draws together people from different traditions.

Further, we must not give the impression that we always want to be in control. The left and other new forces who we want to involve in Respect or whatever develops out of it will not get involved if they see the organisation dominated by the SWP. We must ensure that the structures and methods adopted are always rigorously scrutinised to see if they create an impediment to others getting involved.

Where do we go from here? There are massive opportunities to build a left alternative to New Labour. Respect is only one stage in the process. It may be that Respect grows and attracts new forces. It may be that Respect takes its forces into some new formation involving left trade unionists and others. The actual line of development cannot be predicted in advance. We need to be attuned and sensitive to opportunities as they emerge. We must be quick and adept in responding. We must also initiate approaches to others.

In all this our approach should be: "firm in principle, flexible in tactics". In that way we will build the left without compromising our revolutionary integrity.

KEEPING A SENSE OF PROPORTION

The following document was written by Kevin Ovenden on 22 October for the SWP's Pre-conference Internal Bulletin. Events have moved on since then, including Kevin's expulsion from the SWP. Kevin Ovenden works in George Galloway's office. He is the author of Malcolm X: Socialism and Black Nationalism.

The debate inside the SWP, Respect and the wider movement sparked by George Galloway's letter to its National Council members on 23 August was always going to bring difficulties.

But I believe the response of the Central Committee (CC) has compounded those difficulties. In particular, the characterisation of the argument as the opening shot in a fundamental battle between "left and right" in Respect, with a right wing bloc supposedly attempting to crush or subordinate the socialist left threatens to widen divisions in the coalition to breaking point.

The CC indicated its response to the Galloway letter at a London caucus on 19 August – four days before anyone had seen it. The position was that Galloway's anticipated call for a

national organiser in Respect was unacceptable if that person was to work alongside rather than below John Rees, and that the unseen letter was an attack on the SWP with the aim of shifting Respect to the right. Six weeks later, party members joined everyone else on the Respect National Council in voting for a national organiser working alongside John Rees. At the same meeting George Galloway and Salma Yaqoob were part of the unanimous vote for a resolution (moved by the representative of the other revolutionary socialist group in Respect) which, among other things, stressed the left wing and socialist character of the coalition.

We have now agreed to Galloway's once unacceptable organiser proposal, and the forces we say are attempting to subordinate the socialist left in Respect are cooperating more closely than ever before with those who emphasise Respect's socialist content.

Something is wrong with the analysis of the past six weeks. We should change it. Doing so raises a range of questions about the party's work. They should be addressed in the course of the discussion period up to our conference in January.

But in the immediacy we should recognise the mistaken course in response to Galloway's letter, and change tack.

It is true that Galloway's letter, not the actions of the SWP, precipitated the argument. But there is no political value whatsoever in saying "he started it". We are a revolutionary socialist organisation which should see further and operate more stably than our allies in any united front or area of work.

But instead of keeping matters in proportion, the CC reaction, to what was admittedly a very difficult meeting with George Galloway, Salma Yaqoob and others on 4 September, was exaggerated.

Rapidly, the position the CC adopted and fought for in the party was that Galloway had made an electoral calculation that he needed "Muslim votes" and, with the possible imminence of the general election, he had formed a bloc with right wing and "communalist" (or soft on communalist) forces which necessitated him launching an attack on socialists in Respect and the SWP in particular.

The argument is wrong and does not stand up to serious examination. The one piece of documentary evidence the CC produced for its interpretation was an article in the East London Advertiser, the local paper in Tower Hamlets. It was held up at the London aggregate on 7 September as an authoritative indication the Galloway's intentions were as the CC claimed. There is also reference to the article in the CC's written response to Galloway.

But the article was not authoritative. The journalist who wrote it got his steer from comments on a sectarian website; not, as the CC intimated, via some briefing from Galloway's staff. The CC was provided with all the relevant evidence of this on 10 September.

Other false arguments have been very damaging. Galloway's letter criticises the fact that the trade union conference, organised by Respect in November last year, lost £5,000 (a shortfall reported at the time to the Respect national officers group but made good seven months later with an unsolicited individual donation in June of this year). He also said it was debatable whether the conference was the right overriding priority for Respect.

Now, these things are debatable. And debating them does not equate to attacking Respect's involvement in trade union work. Raising questions about a conference is not equivalent to downplaying working class politics. There are important figures in Respect with vast trade union experience who also raise questions about the Organising for Fighting Unions initiative. It would be absurd to claim they are anti-union or are moving away from class politics to appease petit bourgeois Muslim businessmen.

It's equally absurd to claim the same about Galloway. Before he wrote his letter to the Respect NC he was on the postal workers' picket lines; after, he wrote a letter – turned into a leaflet – co-signed by Lindsey German, Abjol Miah and Shaheed Ali, the leader and deputy leader of the Respect group on Tower Hamlets council, supported the Metronet strikers who brought the tube to a standstill. Galloway has spoken out in support of the prison officers walkout; he has had striking workers on his radio show; he has invited the deputy general secretary of the CWU and the general secretary of the POA onto the show; and more besides. None of this deserves plaudits – it's what we should expect. But none of it is evidence of a supposed shift away from trade unionism in order to placate businessmen.

It is similar when it comes to Galloway's questioning of money spent on Respect's Gay Pride intervention. Questioning the amount spent and complaining about the failure to publicise the intervention having spent that money, might be right or wrong. It is not, however, "pandering to homophobia". Before Galloway's letter to the Respect NC he wrote solidarity statements to the NUS LGBT conference and to the Student Pride demonstration in Manchester; after it, he has spoken out in defence of LGBT rights in the media and on his website.

The CC, however, highlights these parts of Galloway's letter and claims they betray a hidden motive or are subtle signals to socially conservative layers that he is distancing himself from the left for the sake of electoral advantage.

It is an utterly specious argument and it is dangerous. The biggest danger is the underlying political assumption – that Muslims are disproportionately anti-gay and that attacking trade unions will reap electoral support in Tower Hamlets.

We have, rightly, over the last few years systematically resisted those on the "pro-war left" who have sought to use LGBT rights to provide a gloss for Islamophobia. We have done so in articles, in Respect meetings, at Marxism and by arming our comrades – and through them others – with the political arguments around homophobia and Islamophobia that are second to none. The misreading and exaggeration of Galloway's letter threatens to disorient all that.

Does any of this mean there are no political differences or tensions between the various forces in Respect or that the coalition – a successful electoral initiative – does not face electoralist pressures? Of course not. There have been differences since the formation of Respect and we should not expect otherwise. There were electoral pressures in 2005 in Bethnal Green and Bow which were every bit as real as those we face now.

The point is not whether these things exist; it is how we characterise and relate to them. A sense of proportion is everything. Galloway's letter is a product of tensions in Respect and should have been dealt with at that level. It is not an attempt to subordinate or crush the socialist left. Claiming that it is will lead to us getting the tactics of how to deal with the very real differences and debates in Respect wrong.

There is, for example, a real and legitimate debate about Respect's strategy should there be a snap general election. Reading this through the prism of a supposed on going "right-left" battle in Respect will unnecessarily polarise the debate, and produce exactly the deepened divisions the party wants to avoid. We should change tack. That means being more upfront about genuine political differences in Respect, while at the same time doing everything we can to remove the air of factionalism that has developed.

Over the next three months and at conference we will be assessing the party's work and the perspective for the period ahead. There is much to discuss. I believe the period is favourable for us and for building what we have described over the last seven years as a strategic imperative – a radical left formation, a political expression of the radical movements, representative of working people, and a tool to hasten the break up of Labourism.

Our approach in Britain, and as a tendency in Europe, has been to refuse the false choice between not seeking to build such a formation on the one hand, and dissolving revolutionary organisation into a broad party on the other. Nothing – Gordon Brown notwithstanding – has changed in the nature of the period to invalidate that.

Indeed, the neo-liberal offensive Gordon Brown is unleashing means that the prospects for building Respect are promising. But we need to learn from the last year and the last six weeks and get what we do right. We should look forward to working with wider layers of people which will require greater political clarity in the party, a deeper level of tactical and strategic discussion among ourselves and, as Lenin put it, a willingness to patiently explain.

RESPECT AT THE CROSSROADS

The following document was sent on 24 October by National Chair of Respect, Linda Smith, to the Respect office in order for it to be circulated to all Respect National Council members.

A very serious situation has developed inside Respect, in particular over the past two months. It comes at a time when the need for a broad pluralist organisation of the left has never been greater. The political conditions facing Respect today are even more favourable than when we launched the Coalition in January 2004. Millions remain opposed to the war and occupation of Iraq and Afghanistan. Brown has tried to present a different face from Blair, but his support for Bush remains.

Trade union members in key unions like the CWU postal workers union are disgusted with the government. Union members are openly campaigning for the political fund no longer to go to the Labour Party. Where the RMT and the FBU led, other unions will inevitably follow. The RMT are discussing forming their own party and standing their own candidates in the GLA elections next May.

Across the country young people attend political events on issues such as the war, climate change, the arms trade and racism in their thousands. Muslim communities continue to face the lash of popular prejudice. All of these people need a political party, to draw together the growing discontent with the political establishment and especially with New Labour.

Unfortunately, the good work undertaken and achieved by Respect over the last three and a half years is now in danger of being completely undermined by the behaviour of the leadership of the SWP.

On the ground many SWP members have worked alongside other members of Respect to great effect.

However, it has become clear over the last two months, and the last two weeks in particular, that the actions of the SWP leadership imperil the very existence of Respect as a broad, pluralistic and democratic left alternative to New Labour. Since the letter from George Galloway, which echoed some of the criticisms others had been making earlier, was sent to the members of the National Council on August 23, the SWP leadership have demonstrated that they are incapable of engaging in open and frank discussion with those who have disagreements with them.

The chain of events in this crisis is contrary to the ethos which Respect has been seeking to develop and which is reflected in its constitution: "Respect is a broad, open and inclusive organisation…

It is politically pluralistic and will encourage all its members to participate in its campaigns and activities".

George Galloway's letter criticised aspects of the way Respect has been run, and proposed some changes, in particular the appointment of a new post of national organiser to work alongside John Rees, the National Secretary. Behind the national organiser proposal was an attempt to bring more diversity to Respect and to start to restore confidence in the way the national office functioned. This proposal – and indeed the letter itself – was responded to with great hostility by John Rees and the leadership of the SWP, who characterised this as a part of a right wing attack on the left in Respect. Salma Yaqoob's document "Challenges for Respect" refuted this and the outrageous allegations of communalism, which the SWP leadership had raised.

In fact, the real issue is whether Respect develops as a pluralist organ-isation in which no single component part dominates or controls.

The National Council on 22 September unanimously reaffirmed the principle of accountability throughout the organisation, including the elected leadership and elected representatives. The National Organiser issue was debated for several hours by the NC on September 22, adjourned to September 29, where agreement was eventually reached that the post would be of equal status and there was consensus that Nick Wrack take up the post on a temporary basis, if he could.

Following the circulation of an email by John Rees calling for suggestions about the National Organiser's position, Alan Thornett added his support to the proposals from Victoria Brittain and George Galloway that Nick take up the post until conference. Nick was instructed by the SWP Central Committee to withdraw his name. When he refused he was expelled from the SWP. At the same time Kevin Ovenden and Rob Hoveman were instructed by the SWP Central Committee to resign their full-time employment with George Galloway's office. Had they resigned it would have seriously disrupted the work of our only MP's office. When they refused they were also expelled from the SWP.

On Monday 15 October a national officers meeting with a built-in SWP majority voted against Nick taking up the National Organiser's post and set aside the issue until conference. The same meeting voted against appointing Ian Donovan and Ghada Razuki to the Conference Arrangements Committee (CAC). The following night, Tuesday 16 October, there was a meeting of the CAC at which Linda Smith, the national chair of Respect, raised the issue of the constitutionality of the CAC itself (which has never been endorsed by the NC).

She also asked for the membership and financial records of the student members. She was unable to get such records or resolve the problem of the CAC itself. The same night, 16 October, there was a major dispute in Tower Hamlets Respect branch, at which the business of the meeting could not be concluded. Most of the 110 members present on the night left the meeting believing that the issues were to be resolved at a committee meeting to be held two days later. SWP members and a few others stayed behind and purported to vote through a completely unrepresentative list of delegates to the national conference.

At the committee meeting two days later the committee voted to reconvene the all-members meeting to settle the delegate question. The SWP's 10 committee members opposed this and when defeated walked out. Astonishingly, a letter was sent out from the Respect national office at 1.35am that night, containing a "transcript" of the committee meeting with a subject line containing obscenities.

On Friday 119 October attempts were made by the SWP to block the election of delegates in Birmingham. Meanwhile the SWP has sent out a circular instructing its members to get delegated to conference.

The passwords to the membership database and office email have been changed and the National Chair has not been given access to them.

All these actions have struck a huge blow at the unity of Respect and put a legitimate conference in jeopardy.

We are appealing to members of Respect to support us in defending the coalition's plurality. We can no longer allow Respect to be jeopardised by one section.

SIGNATORIES

Linda Smith, National Chair
Cllr Salma Yaqoob, National Vice-Chair
Ken Loach, National Council
Victoria Brittain, National Council
Yvonne Ridley, National Council
Abdurahman Jafar – Muslim Council of Britain
Abdul Khaliq Mian – National Council Member Newham
Clive Searle – National Council Member Manchester
Mobeen Azhar – National Council Member Manchester
Berny Parkes – National Council Member Dorset
John Lister – National Council Member
Nick Wrack, National Council Member
Cllr Abjol Miah, National Council and leader Respect group Tower Hamlets council
Alan Thornett, National Council London
Rita Carter, National Council London
Dr Mohammed Naseem, National Council Member Birmingham
Ger Francis, National Council Member Birmingham
Ayesha Bajwa, National Council Tower Hamlets
George Galloway MP, National Council

Abdul Karim Sheik – Leader of
Respect Group of Councillors
Newham
Hanif – Newham Councillor
Mamun Rashid – Tower Hamlets
Councillor
Abdul Munim – Tower Hamlets
Councillor
Dulal Miah – Tower Hamlets
Councillor
Haroun Miah – Tower Hamlets
Councillor
Fuzol Miah – Tower Hamlets
Councillor
Mohammed Ishtiaq – Birmingham
Councillor

RESPECT IS IN CRISIS – HOW DID WE ARRIVE AT WHERE WE ARE NOW?

To the SWP Central Committee and membership: From Jerry Hicks

Was it George Galloway's letter sent out on 23rd August 2007 to all Respect National Council members, stating some observations, expressing some criticisms and making some suggestions? Or was it the hysterical reaction by the SWP leadership in the weeks that followed? Despite apocalyptical warnings and assertions of "no capitulation" in the SWP road shows that took place in September, virtually all of Galloway's solutions were agreed but only after weeks of vile and damaging blood letting.

On receiving the letter of August 23rd there were two ways of dealing with it. We had a choice to defuse or to ignite. We, i.e. the SWP leadership, chose to do the latter and have been fanning the flames ever since.

I attended the Respect National Council meeting 22nd September 2007, where it became evident for the first time to the overwhelming majority of the council that there

have been very serious and deeply disturbing problems for nearly two years.

Every end has a beginning and a number of soul searching questions need to be asked.

As the SWP is by far the single largest organisation in Respect, should it not then shoulder the greatest responsibility to ensure that Respect not only survives but grows, flourishes and prospers?

How can it be that the national Respect membership numbers only 2500 when the SWP membership is nearly 6000. Obviously fewer than a 1/3 of the SWP membership are even in Respect?

When was the last time we as individual members of the SWP took part in a campaign or union activity and identified ourselves as Respect?

When did we bring anyone – friend, family, colleague or supporter of a campaign that we are involved in – to Respect events or activities?

When was the last time as an individual we recruited or even asked anyone to join Respect?

Who is responsible for allowing this when the official line is that the SWP throws its full weight behind Respect?

Why have so many SWP members not even joined Respect, yet are called to go to meetings around the country to discuss Respect and are now being urged to join Respect and to get delegated to Respect conference! See email below sent out on the 17th October 2007.

Respect annual conference

"The Respect annual conference is going to be very important this year. We are urging comrades do the following:

"You can only get delegated to Respect conference if you are a registered member. You MUST be a paid-up member by THIS FRIDAY, 19 October. Deadline for resolutions is Friday 19 October.

"Deadline for the election of delegates is Sunday 4 November. Once again we are urging as many SWP members as possible to get elected to the Respect Conference. If you have any questions please contact John Rees or the SWP National Office. Martin Smith, SWP National Organiser."

We in the SWP also need to ask ourselves the following questions.

Did we play any part in reaching this disastrous situation, or is it all due to George Galloway's letter of August 23rd 2007? When did it all start to go wrong? Was it August 23rd or long before that?

Who or how many knew of the issues? Why was there no debate or discussion within the SWP or Respect National Council immediately problems began to arise to try to resolve the differences and thereby avoid being where we are now?

In my view the responsibility rests with the SWP leadership for this situation of crisis to have been developing over many months, even years, whilst in the SWP we were told nothing.

Is Bristol different and is this only a London thing? Lots of people in Bristol Respect have done lots of things but we only stood for one council seat in this year's May elections. Let's ask ourselves why. Was it because we had grown? Was it because we did not want to stand in any other ward?

Or, was it in part because not enough people in the SWP in Bristol had either joined Respect or done one single thing to help Respect?

Whilst we might not have the upheaval of Tower Hamlets, our own Annual General Meeting (AGM) held on 27th September 2007 was almost ruined by our full time SWP organiser who wanted to call all the SWP members out of the room 5 minutes before the AGM was due to start, leaving non-SWP Respect members (a third of the meeting) sat there not knowing what the hell was going on.

That potential disaster was averted because I refused to let it happen, but it would have without my intervention. Who would bet that this is not happening elsewhere.

Galloway was and is a maverick, warts and all. We all knew this. I am not making excuses, just stating the blindingly obvious. The Big Brother experience was considered by many a mistake, but his performance before the US Senate was unrivalled and made the name of Respect known across the globe. To describe Galloway as right-wing is farcical. To vilify him and demonise him as the enemy, beggars belief.

The 27 members of Respect National Council who are also critical of the SWP do not represent a "Galloway faction" as is being presented, nor are any of them right-wing or witch hunters as we are being asked to believe. They include people like Ken Loach, Linda Smith, Victoria Brittain, Salma Yaqoob and Yvonne Ridley. They are all socialists, they are all remarkable people in their own right and they are all senior members of Respect.

I feel that our SWP leadership has created an atmosphere where an observation made is described as a criticism, where any criticism is taken as an attack, which is transposed as being "right-wing".

Are we really supposed to believe that we were in an "all or nothing", "them and us" situation where everything we the SWP say must be true, and that everything the "other side" says must be lies. Everything we the SWP do is right but everything they do is wrong!

Frankly, as in life or politics this is ludicrous.

After having overreacted to Galloway's letter in August, the SWP leadership rallied its membership to emergency party councils and road shows, seeking votes of endorsements predicated on half truths and contorted facts to justify their position, in a dishonest and degrading manner.

When sound judgement was needed we got poor analysis; when honesty and frankness were required we got a call for blind loyalty and expulsions.

The situation has been appallingly handled by our SWP leadership, with a series of misjudgements eventfully reaching a position of a self fulfilling prophecy.

Have we just thrown away a fantastic opportunity? Are we now dashing the hopes of millions having given others and ourselves a glimpse of what is or was possible?

Was it right that so many were ready to join the chorus of catcalls vilifying some of Respect's brightest stars without more thoroughly questioning the denouncements.

I have seen things that I can no longer accept.

I have heard things from meetings I have been at described in a way that I don't recognise.

No longer will these things be done in my name.

For the reasons that I have set out, as from this moment I am resigning from the SWP.

To those of you who will feel let down, I offer an unreserved apology; to those who will feel disappointed I am truly sorry; to those who could not care less and who may from here on invent their own distorted version, I wish you well in your world.

We all have to live with our own decisions and I know I am leaving the SWP with my integrity and honour intact and feel sure that I will be able to sleep well at night, safe in the knowledge that I did what I did for the right reasons at the right time and with the best intentions.

OUR ANSWER TO THE ALLEGED "WITCH HUNT" IN RESPECT

Dear Respect Member,

Last Friday 26 October a letter titled "Respect Appeal against the witch hunt" went out to all members from the Respect National Office.

We deplore the fact that the letter, which has been circulating through non-Respect channels for a week by the SWP, is titled "Respect appeal against witch-hunting" as though it had some kind of official sanction. It has never been agreed at either the National Executive or the National Council. It is not a "Respect Appeal".

We, as members of the Respect National Council who are not members of the Socialist Workers Party, wish to answer this petition.

There is no witch-hunt against "socialists including the SWP" in Respect.

The letter claims there "is now overwhelming evidence that the democratic structures of Respect are being circumvented and marginalised" and that "some national officers are attempting to unilaterally by-pass the existing democratic structures of Respect and to witch-hunt socialists including the SWP."

No evidence is provided to substantiate these or any of the other claims in the letter.

Unfortunately, it is the SWP leadership which is orchestrating a campaign of misinformation against George Galloway and others of us who disagree with them.

The SWP leadership carried an editorial in last week's edition of their paper Socialist Worker, publicly attacking George Galloway.

At no time has George Galloway or any one of us attacked the SWP in the national media. Regrettably, as a result of the SW editorial, an article about divisions within Respect appeared in yesterday's Observer.

We reject the other accusations made in the letter:

The SWP leadership is attempting to delegate students to the Respect conference where there is no entitlement to these delegates. We have no objection at all to student delegates properly elected according to the constitution.

We completely disagree with the interpretation of events in Tower Hamlets. SWP members there prevented a members' meeting from electing delegates and then purported to elect an unrepresentative list of delegates at an unconstitutional meeting held when the overwhelming majority of members had left.

We no longer have confidence that the conference called for 17/18 November will be validly constituted.

We are shocked that access to the Respect database and

therefore communication to Respect members was denied to the chair, Linda Smith, and the vice-chair, Salma Yaqoob, when the access codes were changed unilaterally by the SWP leadership. Only under pressure has that information been released.

We further deplore the fact that four councillors in Tower Hamlets split from Respect on Thursday evening, a fact they announced in a widely circulated press release. The four include two members of the SWP and two close allies. They are, in fact, the first four signatories to the SWP's 'Respect Appeal against the witch hunt".

Instead of deploring the split by these councillors and asking them to rejoin Respect, SWP members in Tower Hamlets and elsewhere are supporting this step.

We, however, remain absolutely committed to the principles and policies of Respect as contained in our founding statement, subsequent manifestos and conference decisions: Respect, Equality, Socialism, Peace, Environment, Community, Trade Unions.

Yours in solidarity,

Linda Smith, National Chair
Salma Yaqoob, National Vice Chair
Mobeen Azhar, National Council
Ayesha Bajwa, National Council
Victoria Brittain, National Council
Rita Carter, National Council
Ger Francis, National Council
George Galloway MP, National Council
Jerry Hicks, National Council
Abdurahman Jafar, National Council
Abdul Khaliq, National Council
John Lister, National Council
Ken Loach, National Council
Abjol Miah, National Council, Leader of Tower
    Hamlets Respect Councillors Group
Bernie Parkes, National Council
Yvonne Ridley, National Council
Clive Searle, National Council
Alan Thornett, National Council
Nick Wrack, National Council

THE BIG LIE

How the SWP's bureaucratic factionalism is wrecking Respect

Liam Mac Uaid and Phil Hearse

Stop Press. Already this article is out of date. It was written on 28 October, but today (29 October) SWP and Respect national secretary John Rees held a press conference with Tower Hamlets Respect councillors who have resigned the party whip to announce the formation of 'Independent Respect'. In effect, just a couple of weeks before the organisation's national conference, the SWP have split Respect. This is a big defeat for the anti-capitalist left in England and Wales, one which is unnecessary and avoidable. The SWP's determination to keep complete control of Respect has wrecked the organisation. It is depressing to have our views so immediately and dramatically confirmed. The SWP played a significant role in splitting the Scottish Socialist Party and have now split Respect. The SWP have given the British and international left a vivid display of their methods.

No one who supports left unity could be anything other than deeply disheartened by the turn of events inside Respect, which has created a crisis that threatens the future of the organisation. The current crisis is unnecessary and the product of the political line

and methods of organisation of the Socialist Workers Party. The real meaning of the crisis, its roots and underlying dynamics, are however being obscured by the SWP's propaganda offensive, an attempt to whip its own members into line and throw up a smokescreen to fool the left in Britain and internationally. How so?

The crisis was started by a letter from Respect MP George Galloway to members of the National Council on 23 August – a time, it should be remembered, that a general election seemed a short-term possibility. In his letter Galloway drew attention to organisational weaknesses of Respect, the decline of its membership and political life in general, but also to the (not unrelated) lack of accountability of the National Officers, including the Respect national Secretary John Rees. These criticisms reflected those that had been made for several years by supporters of Socialist Resistance. Galloway also made a series of proposals for breathing life back into Respect's campaigning, including an election campaign committee and a National Organiser.

A sensible response by the SWP leadership to these proposals would have been to say "OK, we don't agree with everything you say, but maybe we took our eye off the ball and need to get things going again. Let's discuss this, let's reach a compromise". This was obviously the intelligent way to deal with the crisis and one that could have led to a positive outcome. But it would have meant the SWP sharing some of the decision-making power it wields within the organisation.

Instead the SWP went into battle mode and declared war on Galloway and those who agreed with him. In order to justify this the SWP has thrown up an extraordinary smokescreen to obscure the real nature of the dispute. This reads as follows: George Galloway and those who support him are witch-hunting the left and SWP in particular. This witch-hunt is being led in the name of 'communalist' politics (read 'Islamism'). The democracy of Respect is being undermined by National Council members who are critical of the SWP. To defend democracy and the left means to support the SWP's position.

The SWP leadership has adopted a classic strategy of unprincipled faction fighters: change the subject. In fact the story they tell – of the mother of all conspiracies, an attack on socialism and the left – is highly implausible to anyone who knows the basic facts. Why should just about everyone of the National Council who is not an SWP member of close sympathiser – including some of their own (now expelled) members in addition to well known socialists like Alan Thornett, Ken Loach, Linda Smith, Victoria Brittain and John Lister – suddenly launch an unprincipled attack on socialism and the left in the name of Islamist 'communalism'? The story may play well at internal SWP meetings, but it is a fantasy. The Rees-German-Callinicos leadership have evidently decided that those who control the terms of the debate, win it. Hence the Big Lie.

Real roots of the crisis

As is normal in these situations, there is an accumulation of fractious meetings, especially leading up the Respect conference and the election of delegates, each of which gives rise to organisational charge and counter-charge. But the roots of the crisis do not lie in what happened at this or that meeting. They lie in the whole approach that the SWP have had to Respect.

While Socialist Resistance and others put forward the objective of building a broad left party, the SWP rejected this in the name of building a "united front of a special kind". In effect this would be an electoral front, a political bloc to the left of Labour to be deployed mainly during elections. It would go alongside a series of other 'united fronts' the SWP wanted to build.

Socialist Resistance pointed out two things: first, an organisation mainly deployed at election time would suffer major disadvantages as against parties and party-type formations that had a permanent existence. Political bases in localities are mainly built through long-term campaigning work, which can then be exploited to create an electoral presence.

But this was anathema to the SWP, because the SWP wanted to have simultaneously the existence of Respect and for the SWP to continue most of its campaigning and propaganda in the name of the SWP itself. The SWP, as easily the largest force in Respect, was able to enforce this orientation. But it meant that Respect was robbed of long-term campaigning work and its own propaganda instruments. For example, the SWP bitterly resisted the proposal that Respect should have its own newspaper – because it would get in the way of selling Socialist Worker. De facto the SWP wanted Socialist Worker to be the paper of Respect.

The "united front of a special kind" was not a united front at all, but a political bloc with a comprehensive programme for British society. The SWP's way of organising it however deprived it of any real internal life of its own and any campaigning dynamic outside elections. Thus it was very difficult to raise the profile of Respect in the national political arena in any systematic way. And it is extremely difficult to keep non-SWP members in this kind of formation, in which they can only – occasionally – give out leaflets and act as meeting fodder.

This was a disaster. As the three major parties cleave more and more together in a neoliberal consensus (a project now near completion in the Liberal Democrats), the political space obviously exists to form a party or party-type formation to the left of Labour. It is not at all obvious that there is less space for this in Britain than in other European countries, where relatively successful broad left formations have existed.

The name or the exact form doesn't matter – you don't have to call it a party. But it has to act like one. This cannot be a revolutionary party, for which at the moment a broad political base does not exist, but revolutionaries can play a central role within it. Such a formation does however have to have a systematic anti-neoliberal and anti-capitalist campaigning stance on all the key questions of the day. Because of the central role of electoral politics in advanced capitalist countries, the left appearing there is vitally important, although made much more difficult in Britain by the undemocratic "first past the post" electoral system, which marginalises the extremes.

In the light of the way that the SWP chose to run Respect, it was inevitable that it would see a decline of its membership and a drift away of independents. Any progressive dynamic for Respect was asphyxiated by the dead hand of the SWP and the strict a priori limits they put on its development. It was thus always highly likely that this would lead to a sharp political discussion about the way ahead; this could have been highly productive and strengthened Respect's role and unity. But the SWP interpreted it as a challenge to their authority and control. In effect they said to the others in Respect: you can have Respect on our terms, otherwise forget it.

SWP's role on the left

It's a basic law of politics that influence and opinion count for nothing if they're not organised, given coherent expression and deployed effectively in society. In Britain there is massive opposition to the war in Iraq and Afghanistan, to privatisation, to the growing gap between rich and poor, to the assault on public services, to the massive enrichment of the City, asset strippers and supermarket capitalists – to neoliberalism as a whole. But this is crying out for political expression at a national level. The fiasco of the failed attempt by the Labour left to get a candidate nominated by MPs in the Labour leadership (non-)contest, illustrates the blocking of any road to the left inside the Labour Party.

Unfortunately the consensus of the three main parties is today more effectively challenged from the right, by the UK Independence party and the fascist BNP; and it was only ever given very partial expression from the left by Respect. Regrettably a more effective attempt to organise left-wing opinion, the Scottish Socialist Party, has for the moment been shipwrecked by the Sheridan crisis – in which, it must be added, the SWP played a terrible role.

Respect is the third major attempt to build a united left formation in the last 15 years – preceded by the Socialist Labour Party (SLP) launched by Arthur Scargill in 1994 and the Socialist Alliance refounded at the beginning of this decade. The SLP foundered on Scargill's insistence on his own bureaucratic control, and the Socialist Alliance's potential was far from maximized: indeed the SWP's decision to sideline the SA during the height of the anti-war movement effectively sealed its fate.

If Respect now crashes this will have extremely negative effects. It will create deep scepticism about the possibility of greater left unity and the potential for a broad left party. It will set back and complicate the whole process of politic-ally and organisationally refounding the British left. Although the SWP leadership clearly don't see this, it will have major negative consequences for the SWP itself, and confirm the suspicions of all those who see the SWP as a deeply sectarian and factional formation.

It will confirm those suspicions because they are, sadly, correct. The SWP, under its present leadership, has shown itself in successive experiences – the Socialist Alliance, the SSP and Respect – to be incapable of fruitful long-term co-operation with other socialists in building a national political alternative. The leopard hasn't changed its spots.

A LETTER TO ALL MEMBERS OF THE SWP (BRITAIN)

Dear comrades,

Your comrades in the International Socialist Tendency in Socialist Worker – New Zealand, have watched what appears to be the unfolding disengagement of the Socialist Workers Party (Britain) from RESPECT – the Unity Coalition, with gradually mounting concern, anxiety and frustration.

SW-NZ's perspective since 2002 has been that building new broad forces to the left of the social liberal (formerly social democratic) parties is an essential step towards the rebirth of a serious anti-capitalist worker's movement. The work carried out by the SWP and its allies to build a broad coalition of the left which could compete with Blairite/Brownite New Labour on equal terms has been an inspiration to us, and, we believe, to all serious socialists throughout the world.

In the last two months, to our distress, all the good work that has been carried out in England and Wales seems on the verge of going down the tubes. Whatever the rights and wrongs of the specific organizational proposals put to the Respect National Council by George Galloway MP in August, an outright civil war has broken out between the SWP leadership and other forces in Respect. This, as far as we can see, could – and should – have been avoided.

It seems to us that your party's leadership has decided to draw "battle lines" between itself and the rest of Respect – a stance, we believe, guaranteed to destroy the trust and working relationships on which any broad political coalition stands. Of particular concern to us is the expulsion of three respected cadre from the SWP – Kevin Ovenden, Rob Hoveman and Nick Wrack – for refusing to cut working relationships with those seen as being opposed to the SWP. To draw hard lines against other forces within a united front (even of a "special type") and to expel members who refuse to accept those hard lines is behaviour you would usually see from a sectarian organization, not a party of serious socialists looking to build a new left alternative. It is perhaps in this context that Galloway's reported comments about "Leninists" should be understood, rather than as an attempt to exclude revolutionary politics from Respect.

What distresses us particularly is that the above-mentioned comrades were expelled after submitting what seem to us to be thoughtful and critical contributions to your pre-conference Internal Bulletin. If these three comrades are not being victimized for raising a political alternative to the line of the Central Committee, it certainly gives the appearance of such victimization – or even, to use a word which has become common currency recently, witch-hunting.

The opening contribution of the SWP CC to the Internal Bulletin makes a couple of points which seem to us to be particularly problematic in this context. Firstly, the CC state that:

The critics of the SWP's position have organised themselves under the slogan "firm in principles, flexible in tactics". But separating principles and tactics in this way is completely un-Marxist. Tactics derive from principles. Indeed the only way that principles can become effective is if they are embodied in day-to-day tactics.

It seems to us an uncontroversial statement that tactics must be based on much more than principles – a lesson which Lenin himself explained clearly in his famous *"Left-Wing" Communism*. Revolutionary tactics must be based on the objective realities of the time – the level of class consciousness, the balance of forces in society at any given moment, the resources and cadre available to a revolutionary organization. To derive tactics from principles is not the method of scientific socialism, but of a dogmatic or even sectarian approach, that the party is "schoolteacher to the class".

As we see it, the disaster overtaking Respect has been exacerbated by the SWP deriving tactics from principles. The principle is that "the revolutionary party" embodies the correct programme, that it must work as a disciplined unit to win its position, and that there is nothing to learn from reformist or other forces. This feeds into a tactical approach that any threat to the organizational leadership of "the revolutionary party" must be fought using all means at the party's disposal, and those forces who oppose the strategy of the party must be eliminated if they do not accept defeat.

According to the information we have, your party chose not to debate Galloway's proposals openly within Respect first, and tease out the politics behind them. Rather, the SWP leadership first moved to neutralize internal dissent, before coming out fighting in Respect with accusations of "witch-hunting". Instead of leading with the political arguments and winning leadership among the broad left forces in Respect, your leadership seems to have mobilized the party for a civil war waged primarily by organizational or administrative means. Inherent in this drive to defeat Galloway and his allies appears a "for us or against us" approach which seems to leave no room for any possible reconciliation – in effect, ensuring the death of Respect in its current form as a coalition of the broad left and a nascent transitional formation of working-class politics.

An attempt by the SWP to establish dominance by sheer force of numbers at the upcoming Respect conference would, it seems to us, result in a Pyrrhic victory at best. Such a course of action, even if successful, would simply drive out those forces who are opposed to your party's current line and leadership, and reconstitute Respect as a front for SWP electoral activities. We cannot see this as encouraging class consciousness or political consciousness, among the SWP, Respect or broader left forces. On the contrary, it seems almost designed to harden the boundaries of organizational loyalty and the divisions between "the revolutionary party" and other forces – almost the definition of sectarianism. Again, if these stories are true, then Galloway's comments about "Russian dolls" would seem to us – as revolutionary Leninists ourselves – to be fair comment.

Another quotation from your Central Committee's IB contribution which struck us runs as follows:

"Of all the claims made against the SWP's position the argument that Respect must be our "over-arching strategic priority" must be the most ill considered. Firstly, it ignores the fact that the building of a revolutionary party is the over-arching priority for any revolutionary Marxist. All other strategic decisions are subordinate to this goal."

Six years ago, the American International Socialist Organisation was criticized by the SWP (Britain) for a sectarian refusal to engage with the anti-capitalist movement. Alex Callinicos' own article on the split with the ISO-US includes the following statement:

In an extraordinary speech at the ISO's convention in December 2000, the group's National Organizer, Sharon Smith, attacked the idea that the ISO could, by systematically focusing on this minority, "leapfrog" over the rest of the left, and insisted that methods of party-building forged in the downturn were necessary irrespective of the changing objective conditions. "Branches are now and will always be the measure of the size of the organization," she said.

The ISO-US was criticized for failing to see that the gains from a revolutionary organization engaging properly in a broad movement, for both the organization and the class struggle, could not be simply quantified by how many members the organization gained. A sect with many members is of far less consequence in the class struggle than a smaller group of revolutionaries playing an organic leadership role in promoting political consciousness among the working classes and oppressed layers. We feel that the SWP may repeat the ISO-US's mistakes – with the much greater consequences, this time, of the wreck of the biggest advance for the British left-of-Labour since the Second World War – if it lets Respect, as "only or primarily an electoral project" crumble at this point.

In contrast, Socialist Worker – New Zealand sees Respect – and other "broad left" formations, such as Die Linke in Germany, the Left Bloc in Portugal, the PSUV in Venezuela and RAM in New Zealand – as transitional formations, in the sense that Trotsky would have understood. In programme and organization, they must "meet the class half-way" – to provide a dialectical unity between revolutionary principle and reformist mass consciousness. If they have an electoral orientation, we must face the fact that this cannot be avoided at this historical point. Lenin said in *"Left-Wing" Communism* that parliamentary politics are not yet obsolete as far as the mass of the class are concerned – this is not less true in 2007 than it was in 1921. The question is not whether Respect should go in a "socialist" or "electoralist" direction, but in how Respect's electoral programme and strategy can embody a set of transitional demands which intersect with the existing electoralist consciousness of the working class.

The personality of George Galloway MP and the links with Muslim communities in London and Birmingham, seen in this light, are surely assets to be worked with, not embarrassments to be minimized. When Galloway came to New Zealand in July to support our campaign against Islamophobia, he electrified audiences with frankly some of the best political oratory that we have ever heard. No-one is claiming that he is a saint, or that he has not made some questionable political choices, but we refuse to believe that somehow over the space of a few months he has become a "communalist, electoralist" devil.

The latest news that comes to us is that John Rees, a SWP CC member and the National Secretary of Respect, has publicly supported the four Respect councillors in Tower Hamlets who have resigned the Respect whip. If this is true, then the "civil war" in Respect has escalated to the point where the two factions are virtually functioning as separate parties – a "de facto" split much more harmful in practice than a clean divorce. This course of action is not only causing a serious haemorrhaging of cadre, but destroying the credibility which your party has built up as the most consistent and hard-working advocate of a new broad left in England and Wales. If the SWP appears to be attempting to permanently factionalise Respect, then it will be no wonder that other forces are trying to exclude them – not because of a "witch-hunt against socialists" (are you seriously claiming that Alan Thornett and Jerry Hicks are witch-hunting socialists?) but for reasons of simple self-preservation.

Socialist Worker – New Zealand comrades see this course of action from our IST comrades in the SWP as potentially suicidal. We see uncomfortable parallels with the self-destruction of the Alliance in New Zealand in 2001-2, where one faction deliberately escalated an inner-party conflict to the point where a peaceable resolution became impossible. Both sides of that struggle were permanently crippled in the aftermath. If you comrades are serious about trying to salvage the potential of Respect, I would urge your party to adopt the following measures:

lower the temperature of the internal struggle in Respect, by agreeing to a postponement of the Respect conference until at least after the SWP conference in January;

recommit to building Respect as an active, campaigning organization in the unions and the movements, rather than a formation solely concerned with fighting elections, and to combining the SWP's work as an independent revolutionary organization with this goal;

put up proposals for more com-prehensive institutions of democratic debate and political education within Respect;

retreat from the current course of factionalist brinkmanship in the current debate, and take whatever steps are necessary to repair the working relationship between yourselves and other leaders and tendencies within Respect; and

retract the expulsions of Kevin Ovenden, Nick Wrack and Rob Hoveman, at least pending debate at your party conference.

If, on the other hand, Respect is finished as a united political force, it would surely be better for the two sides in this debate to approach the question of "divorce" amicably and calmly, rather than forcing the issue to a final conflict in the next few weeks and destroying the trust between the SWP and other forces on the left for perhaps a long time.

I would also encourage your party to, as a matter of urgency, write a report for the information of your fellow members of the International Socialist Tendency, giving your analysis of the crisis within Respect and your long-term strategy for building a broad-left political alternative in Britain.

In solidarity,

Daphne Lawless
Editor, UNITY magazine
Socialist Worker – New Zealand

31 October 2007

BOLSHEVIKS AND RESPECT: OPEN LETTER TO MANCHESTER SWP

Roy Wilkes

Comrades,

Thank you for organising Thursday's public meeting on the 90th Anniversary of the Russian Revolution, something which is well worth celebrating.

Both Chris Nineham and Colin Barker mentioned some of the disagreements that had wracked the Bolshevik party during 1917. If anything, they understated the extent of those disagreements. The entire central committee maintained, prior to Lenin's return in April, that socialist revolution simply wasn't on the cards in Russia, at least until such time as capitalism had been allowed to develop the productive forces, and hence the relative social weight of the working class. As Chris pointed out, the majority of the population were peasants, and the economy was the most backward in Europe.

Trotsky had developed a different analysis, based on his experiences in 1905. But of course he wasn't a member of the Bolsheviks at that time, and only joined the party after Lenin's return. Trotsky argued that the bourgeoisie was incapable of carrying out even the democratic tasks of its own revolution, that the role of leadership fell to the working class (at the head of the peasantry) and that in taking power the workers would not halt the revolution at its bourgeois democratic stage, but would allow it to pass over uninterruptedly into a socialist revolution (i.e. in the words of Marx, one that would make despotic inroads into private property.) In response to the central committee's conservativeness, Lenin wrote the *April Theses*, which agreed in essence with Trotsky's analysis. He was even prepared to break discipline in order to appeal over the heads of the central committee to the most advanced workers.

Was Lenin threatened with expulsion for this indiscipline? Of course he wasn't.

By October, after Lenin had won a majority, there were Bolsheviks who argued publicly against the insurrection. Were even these comrades expelled? No they were not.

Nor did the Bolsheviks always vote rigidly as a bloc within the soviets. The disciplined democratic centralism of the Bolsheviks, which is so poorly understood by many of those who describe themselves as Leninists, has to be understood, not in the abstract, but in the real historical context in which it operated, i.e. as a means of defending the party from a highly repressive Tsarist state apparatus. It was not intended as a means of constraining party members to the extent that they would appear as a monolithic bloc within the workers movement.

I am sure the point I am making here has not escaped you, comrades. It is that the Bolsheviks enjoyed a vibrant and dynamic internal life and were exceedingly tolerant of dissent, even when that dissent was expressed publicly.

On the subject of the behaviour of Bolsheviks within the soviets, Colin later remarked that "Some people didn't like the Bolsheviks, just as some people don't like the SWP. Some of them are even here tonight," which of course earned a big laugh. Aside from the fact that such remarks are intended to make people from other tendencies feel uncomfortable and unwelcome, which is disingenuous when you have advertised the meeting as a public one, it does betray an element of paranoia. It's not that we don't like you, comrades; it's that on some issues we sometimes disagree with you. Is that so hard to bear?

And I don't think the analogy between the Bolsheviks and the SWP was entirely accidental either. The entire tenor of the meeting seemed intended to imply that Bolshevik Party = SWP. It is perfectly conceivable that your current may constitute a part of some future mass revolutionary party. But if you actually believe that you are

already there, that the SWP is the last word in Bolshevism, that you can safely insulate yourselves from every other strand of Marxist thinking, that every other Marxist current is wrong and you are right, then quite frankly you are deluding yourselves.

I was also surprised to hear Colin confirm in his speech that your group is clinging to the view that the Soviet Union was state capitalist. Although this simplistic view ("neither Washington nor Moscow") may have helped you in the seventies and eighties to become the largest left group in politically backward Britain (and let's not forget that the largest left group in pre-1914 Russia wasn't the Bolsheviks, it was the Mensheviks), this analysis simply doesn't stand up to any historical scrutiny. Can you still not see that the collapse of the Soviet Union was a catastrophic defeat of the entire working class, not just within its own territory, but globally? What are conditions like now for workers in Uzbekistan, in Kazakhstan, in Russia itself? And how did we get to where we are now, with the most unfavourable balance of forces in living memory, other than via the smashing of the Soviet Union and the subsequent global hegemony of imperialism? An organisation which clings to its old orthodoxy in the face of all the evidence of history has more in common with a religious sect than with the party of Lenin.

These are just some of the issues that we need to discuss and debate, comrades, in an open, serious, mature and comradely manner. That is how we educate ourselves as Marxists. That is how we develop our ideas and our theory. Don't isolate yourselves from the rest of the left in the mistaken belief that isolation will allow you to get on with building the revolutionary party, free from the irritation of people disagreeing with you.

I hope you will take these remarks in the comradely spirit in which they are intended.

RENEWING RESPECT

The following statement has been issued by Linda Smith, National Chair of Respect, and Salma Yaqoob, National Vice-Chair of Respect.

"Respect was founded to bring together people from divergent political backgrounds in a common struggle for peace, equality and justice.

"It is now clear, however, that there is a fundamental and irretrievable breakdown in trust and relations between the SWP leadership and other parts of Respect.

"There can be no confidence in the legitimacy of the forthcoming Respect conference. The entire democratic process in Respect has been corrupted. If the conference goes ahead it will do no more than confirm that the SWP leadership is hijacking Respect for its own factional purposes. We will not be attending it.

"This breakdown in relations has occurred because the SWP leadership arrogantly refuses to countenance any situation in which they are not dominant and do not exercise control. They are determined to put the interests of the SWP above that of Respect.

"The sectarianism and 'control freak' methods of the SWP have led us to a situation where Respect is irretrievably split. The SWP leadership has supported the breakaway of four councillors from the Respect group in Tower Hamlets, who then went into coalition talks with the Liberal Democrats.

"We have no intention of giving up the struggle for a pluralistic, democratic and broad left wing movement. We will therefore be holding a Respect Renewal conference to discuss the future for progressive politics in Britain today. We are confident that this conference will attract a broad range of support from those who are interested in discussing how we can work together in pursuit of common objectives.

"This renewal conference will take place in London on Saturday 17 November, and we urge as many people as possible to attend it.

"Respect, in its current form, cannot continue. But it is in the interests of all us, including those in the wider left and anti-war movements, that this division is carried out in the most amicable manner possible – one that resolves any legal or organisational questions through negotiation.

"Two meetings have taken place between us and the SWP Central Committee, in the presence of an independent chair respected by both sides. The independent chair confirmed to both groups that there was agreement that the relationship had come to an end, and that what we were discussing were proposals for an amicable resolution of any outstanding organisational questions. Just days later, the SWP backed the split in the Respect group on Tower Hamlets council and walked out of further negotiations.

"We remain committed to finding a negotiated solution to these issues. And we understand that the independent person is willing to continue their efforts to bring the two sides together. We urge the SWP to seek to resolve outstanding legal and organisational questions through further negotiations, in the hope that these matters will not have to be resolved elsewhere."

BEYOND FAKE UNITY

Thinking outside the box has polarised Respect

John Lister and Alan Thornett

As events in Respect have spiralled downwards into crisis, various calls for unity have been raised which have a certain superficial attraction. Wouldn't it be better if the two sides of the National Council (basically the SWP and fellow travellers on one side, and everyone else, including recent expellees from the SWP, on the other) could just sort out their differences and work together?

But the idea has had less credibility by the hour: the actions of the SWP and its immediate supporters (in response to a crisis entirely of their own making) have been so damaging, so cynical and so reckless that it is now impossible to find a core of members of the National Council who would be willing to trust them to honour any agreement that might be proposed.

We already have the experience to show that these fears are well founded.

This is not the first time around for a unity drive: after the acrimony of the 22 September NC in which 13 out of 14 SWP speakers had personally attacked George Galloway, seemingly determined to force him out of Respect, before moving on to pass, in his absence, some of the key proposals from his August letter to the National Council, peace appeared to break out. The 29 September National Council carried a succession of unanimous votes for unity.

The NC:

...voted unanimously – on a motion proposed by an SWP member – to press George Galloway to reconsider his resignation as parliamentary candidate and to come back into a leading role in Respect;

... voted unanimously for a formula which would allow the appointment of a national organiser to work alongside John Rees;

... voted unanimously to endorse a resolution to conference originally written by Alan Thornett and John Lister, but moved at the meeting by Alan Thornett jointly with John Rees. This included a number of proposals which for three years had been points of contention, including agreement in principle to launch a newspaper.

There was also an apparent con-sensus of the vast majority of delegates in proposing that Nick Wrack, then still in the SWP, should be nominated to the national organiser post.

It's worth recalling these slightly surreal discussions and decisions from September 29th, because since then every one of the unanimous decisions has been opposed and obstructed by the SWP leadership and its coterie who voted for them at the time.

The frenzied, back-biting attacks on George Galloway have continued and intensified in closed SWP meetings and in more public arenas. This same process of polarisation has alienated more prominent members of the SWP.

Nick Wrack

Nick Wrack has been hauled before an SWP Star Chamber, instructed to decline nomination for the job as national organiser of Respect (for which he was the only candidate), and expelled when he refused. Rob Hoveman and Kevin Ovenden, long-standing and experienced SWP members working in George Galloway's office, were hauled before a similar SWP committee and instructed to resign their jobs or be expelled: they too have now been expelled from the party. Leading trade union militant Jerry Hicks did not wait to be expelled: he drafted a devastating critique of his party's leadership and resigned from the SWP.

The masquerade of unity was also promptly undermined by polarised meetings in Tower Hamlets, and more recently in other towns and cities, in which the SWP has battled to secure the lion's share of delegate positions for the conference, and hyped up the rhetorical attacks on Galloway, Salma Yaqoob and those who have supported them.

The conflict has not been accidental but deliberate: every clash, and every angry, frustrated statement or expletive that has been provoked, has then in turn been exploited to build up the fiction of a "left-right" clash in Respect, a "witch-hunt" against the SWP – in which all of the various currents and individuals which have criticised the way Respect has been run, and identified with the points made by George Galloway and Salma Yaqoob, have been branded as the "right" wing.

A "petition" against the non-existent witch-hunt has been whipped up as a test of loyalty to hundreds of SWP members up and down the country, many of whom have as a result signed as "Respect supporter", indicating that they are not even members of the organisation.

At the top of the list are the names of four Tower Hamlets councillors, two of them SWP members and two very close to the SWP, who have subsequently held a press conference to publicise their resignation of the Respect whip and the establishment of a new party grouping in Tower Hamlets – Respect (Independent) which may run candidates against Respect. The press conference was arranged by a full time worker in the Respect Office (an SWP member clearly working under the direction of Central Committee member John Rees), with the £300+ venue billed to Respect, and attended by Respect National Secretary John Rees, who has yet to voice any criticism of this very public and very damaging split in the organisation, which has given huge ammunition to New Labour and relegated Respect from its position as the main opposition party in Tower Hamlets.

The SWP leadership has resorted to ridiculous manoeuvres in their efforts to manipulate an artificial majority behind their position at the Respect conference, scheduled for November 17: large numbers of phantom members have been claimed for "Student Respect", an organisation wholly owned and controlled by the SWP, allowing the SWP to send along one delegate for every ten claimed members, and potentially outvote genuine delegates from real branches. When challenged to produce evidence that these students were genuine members, the SWP leadership has responded by claiming this is another part of the "witch hunt" and an attempt to exclude students.

Increasingly acrimonious Respect meetings in different cities are seeing battles over delegations to conference, in several instances leading to more SWP members resigning in disgust at their party's sectarian antics, as well as angry walk-outs by non-SWP members.

Looking over the period since Galloway penned his critical letter at the back end of August, it is impossible to avoid concluding that the SWP leadership's tactics have been an absolute and unmitigated disaster not only for Respect, which can never be restored, but also for the SWP itself.

From the prestige and credibility it gained by acting as the principal organised political current in the most successful political regroupment to the left of Labour since World War 2, the SWP leadership has now cemented itself into the position of a rigidly centralist and dogmatically sectarian current that would rather smash three years' work and destroy hard-won political alliances than tolerate any genuine pluralism or political development in Respect.

All of the worst fears and reservations so widely held on the left about the SWP and its methods have been confirmed: the Party's line has been so appalling that its every tactic appears designed to demoralise its best members, alienate non-SWP members and further isolate the party within Respect.

Even their very worst enemies could not have hatched up a scheme half as destructive as the one the SWP Central Committee has imposed upon itself. It must be the first time such a large-scale left current effectively launched a witch-hunt on itself, driving towards a split which – if they were to go to a stitched-up Respect conference and win the vote – would be a Pyrrhic victory, leaving only a downsized SWP and a wafer thin layer of hangers-on in Respect.

Such a formation would never attract any broader forces – many of whom will instinctively recoil from the SWP for years to come as the reality becomes more widely known.

The SWP leadership have also broken from most of the well-known figures who could draw a crowd for Respect – notably Galloway and Salma Yaqoob, but also Victoria Brittain and Ken Loach.

In other words the SWP leadership's tactics have driven off virtually all of the independent forces that made Respect a genuinely broad-based coalition.

After three years of work they now stand to walk away from the project weaker and more discredited than they were before it launched: their track record is one of politically hobbling Respect, under-selling it and failing to tap its potential in a period uniquely favourable to building a left alternative. And having failed to build it to its potential, rather than face up to any of the errors that have been made, or correct them, they have embarked on a suicidal policy of polarising Respect for and against the SWP.

However, for those of us who have not stopped looking to build a broad left-wing party, the fact that the SWP leadership appears to have pressed the self-destruct button opens up a far from a satisfying situation. They are threatening to destroy something far more than the SWP itself.

The problem is that if the SWP leadership stick to their guns, reject the proposals that we have made for postponement, and insist on convening the conference on November 17, there is no viable basis for non-SWP members to participate in it. There could only be a negative outcome.

We already know that there is no way we would be allowed to win any votes, and that the process of checking credentials of delegations from Tower Hamlets, Student Respect and other areas would be a nightmare, with a real possibility of anger and frustration on both sides exploding into threats and even violence.

But we also know that even if by some fluke we *did* win a vote on a contested issue, there is no chance of the policy being implemented as long as the SWP leadership calls the shots.

Worse, we know from grim episodes in the history of the sectarian left, and from the way the SWP has now drummed up signatures for its current "petition", that it is possible for highly centralised groups such as the SWP to march in squads of delegates who know what they are going to vote for before they get there, and will be oblivious to the damage that they and their antics do to the organisation.

We also know the impact a polarised, packed conference like this would have on independent forces and those with no experience of the far left: they would be profoundly shocked, alienated and demoralised. The result would be that many valuable people would be lost to the project and quite possibly lost to the left for years to come.

So we have a real problem: do we march whoever we can gather into a stitched-up conference to be abused and reviled and voted down by SWPers accusing us of witch-hunting them – and decide only afterwards how to regroup and rebuild?

Do we participate in a conference that not only cannot solve the problems, but which could make them many times worse and also parade them on the national stage in front of the press and mass media, to the delight of the real right wing and witch hunters?

Or do we decide that that is a not a useful expenditure of energy, and that the time has come to build something new and inclusive which can address the problem of working class representation for which Respect was originally launched to address?

Of course it would be a setback to accept that Respect as we have known it, with all the effort involved in getting it off the ground, had been destroyed by the SWP leadership. But the fact is the political conditions which created it are as relevant now as they were then, even more so. And it is already clear that there are people all round the country who are ready to join or rejoin a more inclusive organisation.

With the emergence of Brown, the situation is far worse in the LP than it was when Respect was founded. The possibility of reclaiming Labour for the left is dead in the water. The defeat of the John McDonnell campaign saw the Labour left at it lowest ebb for 60 years. There has to be a recomposition of the left which goes far beyond what Respect has been able to do.

We need a new organisation as soon as possible which will start to address these issues and create the condition to unite with those from the Labour left, the trade union left and the activists of ecological and climate change campaigns which can present a politic alternative to the betrayals of new Labour.

THE END OF RESPECT AS WE KNEW IT...

Alan Thornett

Respect as we have known it for the last four years, based on an alliance between the SWP and George Galloway, is over.

It is a remarkable situation. The SWP leadership has managed to alienate virtually all of the active non-SWP members of the National Council. Among them are Linda Smith, National Chair; Salma Yaqoob, National Vice-Chair; Victoria Brittain, writer and playwright; George Galloway, the Respect MP; Jerry Hicks, leading industrial militant and member of the SWP at the start of this; Ken Loach; Abjol Miah, the leader of Respect on Tower Hamlets Council; Yvonne Ridley, journalist;

Alan Thornett, George Galloway, Salma Yaqoob at Respect Renewal conference, 17 November

Following the decision of the SWP central committee last Wednesday that the Respect conference would go ahead as planned and unchanged – in other words on a completely undemocratic basis – 21 members of the non-SWP part of the National Council have issued a call for an alternative conference on the theme Renew Respect. Work is going ahead to build it on the broadest basis possible.

and Nick Wrack – the first national chair of Respect and a member of the SWP when this debate started.

No other organisation or nationally-known individual has remained with the SWP side in this. Faced with a Respect conference on 17–18 November which is organised on a totally undemocratic basis, and which will have a built-in SWP majority after a campaign by the SWP to pack the conference with its own delegates, members of the National Council have called an alternative conference on 17 November on the theme of "Renew Respect".

Initial speakers include George Galloway MP, Linda Smith, Salma Yaqoob and Ken Loach. It will start the process of rebuilding Respect on a different and more inclusive basis.

The start of the crisis was the SWP's disastrous reaction to a letter from George Galloway to the National Council at the end of August. This raised some home truths about the development of Respect, which some of us had been raising for a long time, and made some modest proposals towards greater plurality. The letter was supportable but did not go far enough. The issue behind it was whether the SWP would relax the tight control which they exerted on Respect and accept some diversity, particularly at the level of the leadership bodies and the national office.

The letter could have opened up an overdue and fruitful discussion about the development of Respect as a more inclusive organisation, with a greater national presence. If the SWP had been prepared to discuss the issues politically, make some compromises – even symbolic compromises – to show that they were prepared to take other people's views into account, and that Respect was not a wholly-owned subsidiary of the SWP, there could have been a positive outcome. Instead they went in totally the opposite direction – confirming that they had no intention of relaxing control.

They took the letter as a frontal attack on the SWP, with all that

implies, and launched a nation-wide tour of SWP districts, vilifying George Galloway and scandalously calling him and Salma Yaqoob (amongst many other things) 'communalists', and characterising the letter as part of a right-wing attack on the left in Respect.

And the George Galloway they were vilifying was the same George Galloway that the SWP had repeatedly shielded from criticism ever since Respect was founded. They now denounced him for unaccountability: yet at the time of the Big Brother debacle, they fought might and main inside Respect to avoid any word of criticism of his unilateral decision to go on the programme, being expressed by Respect.

At the Respect National Council meeting on 22 September the dispute focused on the proposal in the letter for a new post of National Organiser alongside the national secretary. SWP delegates, reflecting their paranoid internal discussions about George Galloway, came close to driving him out of Respect under conditions which would have collapsed Respect ahead of an expected general election.

The meeting ran out of time and adjourned until September 29, when agreement was eventually reached that the post would be of equal status with the National Secretary. There was also a consensus that Nick Wrack, a former national chair of Respect and an SWP member, take up the post on a temporary basis, if possible.

When this was activated Nick Wrack was instructed by the SWP Central Committee to withdraw his name from the frame. When he refused he was expelled from the SWP.

At the same time two workers in George Galloway's office who were members of the SWP were instructed by the SWP Central Committee to resign their jobs. When they refused they were also expelled from the SWP. On Monday 15 October a Respect Executive Committee meeting with an SWP majority voted against Nick taking up the National Organiser's post and set aside the decisions of the NC on the matter. Behind the national organiser issue was the wider issue of whether Respect was to develop as a pluralist organisation in which no single component part dominates or controls, or one controlled at every level by the SWP.

The following night there was a meeting of the Conference Arrange-ments Committee (CAC), at which Linda Smith, the national chair of Respect, raised the issue of the constitutionality of the CAC itself (which has never been endorsed by the NC). She also asked for the membership and financial records of the student members. She was unable to get such records or resolve the problem of the CAC itself.

By now the SWP were presenting the battle inside Respect as a battle of right against left, with themselves being the defenders of the socialist camp inside Respect. This was the same SWP who have always fought to lower the socialist profile of Respect. Publication after publication came out in the name of Respect with the SWP in control without a mention of socialism from cover to cover.

I was one of the first, when the SWP joined the Socialist Alliance in 2000, to say that the turn they had made towards working with others on the left, after many years of isolationism, was an important step forward for the whole of the left. Now after four years of the Socialist Alliance and three and a half years of Respect this turn outwards has effectively come to an end. It is impossible to see the SWP, with its current leadership and method of operation, playing a positive role in the construction of a broad pluralist party in the foreseeable future.

In fact even as this battle for Respect has continued, the SWP leadership have been theorising their exit from this strategy. The first bulletin for the SWP conference (in January) has last-minute CC text (written in the middle of this debate) which argues that the period of the upsurge of struggle in the mid 1990s and through Seattle and into the first years of this century, which created most of the left parties, is starting to wither. Right-wing currents are developing inside these parties – including the current op-position inside Respect.

It is a short step from this to con-cluding that the era of such parties is over and that it is "time to build the party". It is hard to see how the SWP can have its heart in anything it salvages from the mayhem they have created. Other CC documents in the bulletin reinforce and entrench the sterile model the SWP has defended for building Respect. For the first time it is openly argued that Respect is an electoral (united) front for the SWP and that it is perfectly acceptable to deprioritise it between elections and reprioritise it when an election comes along.

This is precisely the model the SWP insisted on imposing on Respect and the model on which it foundered. What this got completely wrong was the relationship between the SWP and Respect itself. This was with the SWP as the dominant organisation with the highest possible public profile and its own press and priorities with Respect as an electoral wing.

More precisely it foundered on the way it conducted democratic centralism inside the SWP and the way this shaped the way they functioned in the broad organisation. This required that the SWP membership would be regimented inside Respect meetings and conferences in a way which alienated everyone else. They would be told what to do and how to vote in advance of meetings and conferences, at caucuses prior to the event. In most cases they were told what to do and how to vote without having been involved in a process of discussion inside Respect itself.

Inside broad left formations there has to be a real, autonomous political life, in which people who are not members of an organised current can have confidence that decisions are not being made behind their backs in a disciplined caucus that will impose its views. They have to be confident that their political contribution can affect political debates. This means that no revolutionary current can have the "disciplined phalanx" concept of operation. Except in the case of the degeneration of a broad left current (as in Brazil) we are not doing entry work or fighting a bureaucratic leadership. This means in most debates, most of the time, members of political currents should have the right to express their own viewpoint irrespective of the majority view in their own current. If this doesn't happen, the real balance of opinion is obscured and democracy negated.

Evidently this shouldn't be the case on decisive questions of the interest of the working class and oppressed, like sending troops to Afghanistan. But if there are differences on issues like that, then membership of a revolutionary current is put in question. Revolutionary tendencies should avoid like the plague attempts to use their organisational weight to impose decisions against everyone else.

That's a disastrous mode of operation in which democracy is a fake. If a revolutionary tendency can't win its opinions in open and democratic debate, unless it involves fundamental questions of the interest of the working class and oppressed, compromises and concessions have to be made. Democracy is a fake if a revolutionary current says "debate is OK, and we'll pack meetings to ensure we win it".

This flawed method is the way the SWP has worked in Respect. It is the polar opposite of the way things must work in a recast and reshaped Respect which emerges out of this crisis.

In *Socialist Resistance* we have long advocated such a method. We supported the way Scottish Militant Labour worked inside the SSP, keeping their own organisation but never intervening in an organisational way inside the SSP. For example they never, under normal circumstances, caucused before an SSP meeting – in order to ensure that they were a part of the process of discussion and not imposing an external discussion.

As the key non-SWP forces within Respect begin to regroup and reorganise, Socialist Resistance will remain as a distinct current within the renewed organisation, but one working honestly and loyally to build the broad organisation and to win support for our political ideas within it, without attempting to manipulate or circumvent the process of democracy and political debate.

RESPECT RENEWAL IS UNDERWAY

Respect, the anti-capitalist left party in England and Wales, has split. Last weekend its two factions held separate conferences. Liam Mac Uaid, editor of Socialist Resistance, explains the roots of the division and the road forward outlined by the Respect Renewal conference.

Origins of the crisis

In August this year Respect's member of parliament (MP) George Galloway wrote a document to the organisation's National Council (NC). At the time it was generally believed that Gordon Brown would announce an early general election and Galloway was clearly alarmed by Respect's utter lack of preparation. Among his key points were:

● Despite being a rather well-known political brand our membership has not grown. And in some areas it has gone into a steep decline.

● We have stumbled from one financial crisis to another.

● With the prospect of an early general election we are simply unable to challenge the major parties in our key constituencies.

● There is a custom of anathem-

atisation in the organisation which is deeply unhealthy.

● There is a marked tendency for decisions made at the national council or avenues signposted for exploration to be left to wither on the vine if they are not deemed to meet priorities.

Respect's National Secretary John Rees is a leading figure in the Socialist Workers Party (SWP). Rees judged the document to be an attack on the SWP. Over the following weeks the SWP claimed that they were being attacked on account of their socialist politics and that a "witch hunt" was being organised against them.

Two camps rapidly formed on the NC. One comprised the SWP members and some allies and the other consisted of Galloway and nineteen non-SWP NC members including International Socialist Group (ISG) members Alan Thornett and John Lister.

The two day annual conference was scheduled for the weekend of 17th and 18 November. It quickly became a major source of contention. The SWP argued that it was the legitimate decision making body and would go ahead as planned. The other camp argued that there was strong evidence from all over the country that SWP branches were being instructed to get as many of their members elected as delegates as they could. In some confirmed cases SWP full timers tried to argue that delegations be comprised entirely of SWP members. Equally controversial was the selection of large numbers of student delegates, many of whom were not paid up Respect members. Another disputed issue was the election of delegates from Tower Hamlets, the borough which contains Galloway's constituency. Two rival delegations each declared the other one illegitimate.

300 attend Renewal launch

The outcome was that on Saturday 17th November both sides of the dispute held separate conferences thus making the split de facto. Each conference attracted about 300 people. Supporters of Socialist Resistance, the paper which the ISG helps produce, attended the Respect Renewal conference. This was the conference which began to organise the majority of non SWP Respect supporters.

TheTheMorningStarnewspaper, which reflects the views of the Communist Party of Britain, said of the audience "The hall was packed out with a genuinely diverse crowd - young and old, men and women, black and white, Asian, Muslim, Christian and those of no faith, plus trade unionists and socialists from different traditions."

Linda Smith, Respect Renewal's chair and an official in the Fire Brigades Union, opened the conference by declaring that it is the real Respect and that the other conference had no legitimacy.

George Galloway in his opening remarks observed that four years after its founding Respect has lost half of its membership and now has only 2500 paid up members. He

argued that the SWP's leadership didn't want Respect to grow too large because they feared they would lose control of a large organisation. Summing up his politics he said "We set out to create a mass, broad party for working people. That party needs pluralism and democracy."

Salma Yaqoob spoke twice. After Galloway she is Respect's best known public figure. She directly referred to the Venezuelan revolution as an example of how some societies are rejecting the neo-liberal model and explained how Respect in Birmingham is trying to build itself as the anti-communalist organisation.

Among the guests addressing the event was Penny Duggan of the Ligue Communiste Revolutionnaire. She reported on the strikes in France and told the audience of the LCR's commitment to building a broad party that will incarnate the resistance to capitalism in France.

Summing up the discussion Nick Wrack remarked on the participants' "feeling of liberation". Even though the organisation had been split down the middle the people in the hall, who formed the core of independent activists and contained significant numbers of Bangladeshi members from Tower Hamlets were determined to carry on building a party. He added that members need to see Respect Renewal as a part of a process towards building a broader party that will include people from the Communist left, the Labour Party and environmentalists. This process will start with a series of meetings and discussions across England and Wales in the coming months with organisations and individuals. George Galloway added that members will be invited to submit documents outlining their ideas on Respect's development and that the acting leadership would be doing the same. There will be a conference after the May elections to develop a programme.

Speaking on behalf of Socialist Resistance John Lister said that the organisation was willing to cease production of its monthly paper and hand over its financial resources as well as its production facilities to allow Respect Renewal to begin producing a monthly paper. This decision was welcomed and agreed by the conference. Socialist Resistance will shortly be discussing how to maintain its own public profile in the light of this step.

Hitting the ground running

The first issue of Respect Renewal's paper will be ready for the Campaign against Climate Change demonstration in December. The new publication will be different from the well designed but uninspiring, apolitical tabloids that Respect has traditionally produced. It will have analysis, discussion and give branches something to organise around.

The split is Respect is a temporary setback in the construction of a class struggle mass party in Britain. However the choice was either a separation or a continuing slow decline. The Respect Renewal conference demonstrated that there are several hundred people who have tried working in Respect for three of four years and have concluded that its old way of working was stopping it from growing. In most parts of the country branches met infrequently or only to elect conference delegates. Many members felt, rightly or wrongly, that the SWP treated it as their own property and felt that the pain and disruption of a split was a necessary price to pay to allow the organisation to develop.

The omens are promising for the relaunched organisation's future. Birmingham, Bristol, Manchester and parts of London sent along enough people to quickly establish viable, dynamic branches. A leadership and infrastructure are emerging quickly. This includes Salma Yacoob, Alan Thornett, Nick Wrack, Rob Hoveman and Kevin Ovenden. These last three were also recently expelled from the SWP.

The conference was a big success. Salma Yaqoob said that she had arrived with a heavy heart but was leaving with a light heart. She had reason to. We were present at the significant next step in the creation of Britain's class struggle, anti-imperialist working class party.

Liam Mac Uaid is an editor of Socialist Resistance and a member of its steering committee. His blog is online at
liammacuaid.wordpress.com

THE 17 NOVEMBER CONFERENCE: A SUMMARY

Nick Wrack

(Note: superscript numbers refer to websites of photos, videos etc, which are listed at the end of this article)

The Respect Renewal Conference was a stunning success.

It took place at the Bishopsgate Institute in the City of London on Saturday 17 November 2007. Notification of the conference had first gone out only on Saturday 3 November. In the intervening two weeks hard work by a team of volunteers ensured a wonderfully uplifting day.

Called at just two week's notice it could have been a desultory affair. Given that it came after an acrimonious split in Respect it could have been rather depressing. Instead, it was a lively, if at times unpredictable, event attended by over 350 people. [A full credentials report will appear soon.]

As the Morning Star reported (Monday November 19), "The hall was packed out with a genuinely diverse crowd – young and old, men and women, black and white, Asian, Muslim, Christian and those of no faith, plus trade unionists and socialists from different traditions."

People came from all over the country, with significant delegations from Tower Hamlets, Newham, Waltham Forest, Dorset, Manchester and Bristol. Birmingham brought a coach load.

The hall was decorated with banners and photographs showing

Respect's successes and from the anti-war movement. Stalls from various left-wing campaigns hugged the walls of the conference hall. A tremendously inspiring video display projected onto the back of the stage images of working-class struggles from the last hundred years.

Behind the scenes a large army of volunteers ensured that the conference was properly prepared and ran smoothly.

There were two cameras video-recording events[1] and several photographers taking pictures[2].

At many times throughout the day there was standing room only. Refreshments prepared by a fantastic team of volunteers kept everyone going. A marvellous cake[3] was eaten by everyone at the end.

When George Galloway's letter[4] to the Respect National Council, containing criticisms about the administration and organisation of Respect, was sent out on August 23 no-one could have predicted that we would end up, just twelve weeks later, with two conferences being held on the same day. No-one could have predicted, and no-one surely wanted, the split in Respect that has taken place.

However, the way in which the dispute was conducted by the leadership of the Socialist Workers Party meant that this split became inevitable. This was recognised by the SWP leadership itself and they entered into negotiations to separate.[5]

It was an irony that the Respect Renewal Conference was taking place in the Bishopsgate Institute. This was the venue where the four breakaway councillors who had resigned the Respect whip in Tower Hamlets held their press conference on Monday 29 October.[6]

That press conference was organised and attended by John Rees, SWP Central Committee member and National Secretary of Respect. This was one of the key events in the developing division, with the SWP leadership condoning and encouraging a split in the Respect group on Tower Hamlets council.

It's been a pretty unpleasant three months for most of us as we have watched Respect split asunder. This split could have been avoided, if only the SWP leadership had been prepared to discuss criticisms and implement agreed compromises. Instead, at each stage it has increased the temperature of the debate, refusing to implement compromise decisions of the Respect National Council, illegitimately ruling out valid delegations to conference while ruling in other invalid delegates and vilifying those who disagreed with it.

Ludicrous claims of a witch-hunt against the SWP are still being made, despite the involvement of many prominent socialists in the Renewal conference. Criticism, even were it unwarranted, does not make a witch-hunt. The political justification for this by the SWP leadership is that there is a left-right split taking place. Again, this will come as a surprise to those at the Respect Renewal conference who will all identify themselves as being on the left.

A political split on the left is seldom good for either side. It can reinforce the idea that the left cannot be unified, that minor differences always outweigh agreement on bigger issues.

We recognise that this split is a set-back. However, there was a sense of liberation at the Renewal conference which reflected a feeling that we can now get on and do many of the things we should have been doing over the last three years – building branches across the country, linking up with others on the left and promoting our image and politics to a much wider audience.

The spirit of optimism and enthusiasm was demonstrated

by the response to the financial appeal in which over £2,000 was collected. This was on top of the registration fee and travel costs that people had already had to pay. Membership forms and standing order forms for Respect Renewal Conference were also filled in or taken away.

There were many speeches, both from the floor and from the platform, which expressed the frustration that Respect's development had been held back by the controlling hand of the SWP leadership. This is because of the SWP's approach towards Respect, which sees it as something to be turned on for elections (in very few places) and then turned off. Those attending the Renewal Conference were very much of the view that Respect needs to be built continuously and broadly across the country. It has to contest elections but it has to be more than solely an electoral organisation. In order to win elections you have to be active and present all the time in between elections.

It is clear that Respect Renewal represents the overwhelming majority of non-SWP members in Respect. Our disagreement has not been with the many SWP members who have worked hard to build Respect but with the SWP leadership, whose political approach and behaviour over the last three months has alienated most of those outside the SWP and, indeed, many within it.

The conference was opened by Linda Smith, Respect National Chair.

Because of her position as chair, Linda has headed up the list of 19 National Council members who have opposed the bureaucratic methods of the SWP leadership. She has also had to suffer a campaign of vilification from some members of the SWP in an attempt to undermine her.

George Galloway, Respect's only MP, introduced the first session with one of his usual tours de force.[7] A great way to start conference. He outlined the reasons the Renewal Conference had been called and answered some of the ridiculous charges that the SWP leadership have levelled against him and others on the Renewal side. He poured scorn on the idea that this was a left-right split, or that he was anti-trade union.

Salma Yaqoob, Respect National Vice-Chair, spoke.[8]

She outlined her opposition to free market capitalism and the idea that there is no alternative to it. She explained how US capitalism relied on its massive military might to dominate economically. She repudiated the charge of 'communalism' made against her by the leaders of the SWP, outlining the practical steps she and other Respect supporters have taken in Birmingham to overcome tensions between different communities.

Ken Loach, world-renowned film director and winner of the Palme d'or, calmly outlined some of the reasons for the split and offered some suggestions for the way forward.

Guest speakers Andrew Murray,[9] Chair of the Stop the War Coalition and Sami Ramadani,[10] Iraqi Democrats against the Occupation, spoke about the need to continue our opposition against the war and occupations and to remain vigilant about further military actions. They both correctly warned about the importance of the split in Respect not being carried into the Stop the War movement and weakening it.

Anas as-Tikriti, from the British Muslim Initiative, reminded conference that he had relinquished his position as chair of the Muslim Association of Britain in 2004 in order to head Respect's list in Yorkshire for the European elections. He is one of many talents that Respect has not called on in recent years.

Throughout the day there were many speakers from the floor. They spoke about the reasons for the split and about how to go forward. Inevitably, there were many contributions that dealt with the role of the SWP leadership. Several of these were all the more powerful because they were made by people who have recently resigned from the SWP: sacked union militant Jerry Hicks gave the most impassioned speech, along with Jo Benefield (35 years in the SWP), Richard Searle, Kay Phillips and Nadir Ahmed, a young member from Newham who resigned from the SWP during his speech.

The presence of these and other former members of the SWP should be answer enough to the suggestion that Renewal is right-wing or anti-trade union.

The SWP leadership were given the opportunity to put their case, with Weyman Bennett and Michael Bradley, both members of the SWP Central Committee, called in to address conference. They were listened to politely.

We were very pleased to have Derek Wall, principal male speaker of the Green Party addressing conference in a personal capacity, together with Hilary Wainwright, editor of Red Pepper. We look forward to working with Derek and others from the radical environmental movement in the future. We hope that we can reach out with Red Pepper to the many thousands of unaffiliated people on the left, to work together on the many issues that concern us all.

One of the silliest arguments made by the SWP leadership against those at the Renewal conference is that we reflect the right of Respect. It was amusing to watch the SWP-Respect conference systematically ask each of the speakers that had agreed to speak at the Renewal conference to speak at theirs. This included Andrew Murray, Sami Ramadani and Derek Wall, who quite rightly took up the invitation to speak at both conferences. Derek's comments on the two conferences can be found at the end of this article.[11]

Derek Wall makes the amusing point that Rania Khan, speaking at the SWP-Respect conference, attacked the Renewal conference for having Derek speaking at it – only then to learn that he was speaking at her conference as well.

Brian Caton, General Secretary of the Prison Officers Association, one of the more militant of British trade unions, sent greetings and best wishes to the conference but Nick Wrack stupidly forgot to pass them on.

Several of our councillors spoke. Mohammed Ishtiaq councillor for the Birmingham Sparkbrook ward answered the charge of communalism by explaining that one of his opponents had come from the same village as his family. People had tried to persuade him not to stand against this person but he had stuck to his guns because it was a matter of policies for him, not family or village.

Three councillors from east London who haven't normally been put on Respect public platforms until now revealed their tremendous abilities, which will no longer be hidden. Councillors Sheikh and Hanif from Newham spoke. Councillor Abjol Miah, leader of the councillors group in Tower Hamlets addressed conference with a powerful speech, showing his prowess as a speaker and his politics as being clearly on the left.

Patricia Armani da Silva, the cousin of Jean Charles de Menezes, who was brutally murdered by the police on 22 July 2005 spoke about the campaign to get justice for Jean. She called for the resignation of Metropolitan Police chief Ian Blair, a demand that was unanimously endorsed by conference.

Francisco from the Venezuela Information Campaign and Penny Duggan from the French League

Comuniste Revolutionnaire (LCR) both addressed key international issues and added an important international dimension to the day. Pakistani lawyer and veteran socialist Anwar Dholan spoke from the floor about the state of emergency and repression in Pakistan.

In the final session National Council members Alan Thornett and Nick Wrack[12] mapped out the way forward for Respect Renewal supporters. Conference endorsed proposals that the 19 National Council members who had called the conference continue to co-ordinate Respect Renewal work over the next six months, along with volunteers who want to help to organise things.

There will be a series of rallies and smaller meetings across England and Wales to discuss and debate the way forward, culminating in a recalled conference either in the Spring or after the May elections next year. Everyone who wants to contribute to the debate will be welcome.

One of the most important announcements was that the Socialist Resistance group, whose members had played a prominent part in building this conference, have agreed to hand over their paper to Respect Renewal. The first edition will appear in time for the Climate Change demonstration on 8 December.

The main message from this conference is that the task of building Respect and the broader opposition to New Labour continues. Of course, there are weaknesses. Emerging from a split means that we have only the skeletal outline of an organisation in most places outside east London and Birmingham. Although there were significant contingents of young Asian men and women from east London and Birmingham,[13] we do not have anything like as many young people as we want. We need to reach out to young workers. We need to begin work in the further education colleges and universities to recruit students. This work will now begin. There are very few African and African-Caribbean members of Respect and we need to address this issue urgently.

Respect is not the finished article – far from it. We are just one small part of the process of building a new party to represent working class people. We have had fantastic successes in Respect's short existence, with the election of an MP and several councillors. But that cannot be enough.

We want to build Respect Renewal. But we also want to reach out to everyone else who wants to build a left alternative to New Labour, the Lib Dems and the Tories. We want to build a bigger, broader and more unified party of the left, representing the desire of working-class people for change. That is our main task: to work with others to create a radical, left party for all, whatever background or tradition. We have energy, enthusiasm, optimism and – most importantly of all – we have the radical, left-wing politics to appeal to millions.

If you want to join or find out more about Respect Renewal then contact us:
http://respectrenewal.org/index.php?option=com_contact&Itemid=3

WEBSITE REFERENCES

1   http://vids.myspace.com/index.cfm?fuseaction=vids.showvids&friendID=163095405&n=163095405&MyToken=3616ba80-ab8a-422c-bb18-b4d6b298081e
2   http://www.flickr.com/photos/eventful/sets/72157603225002002/
http://www.flickr.com/photos/eventful/sets/72157603225002002/show/
http://marxsite.com/rspectrenewphoto.html
3   http://www.flickr.com/photos/eventful/2044120430/in/set-72157603225002002/
4   http://www.socialistunity.com/?p=726
5   http://www.socialistunity.com/?p=1024
6   http://www.eastlondonadvertiser.co.uk/content/towerhamlets/advertiser/trialbyjeory/story.aspx?brand=ELAOnline&category=trialbyjeory&tBrand=ELAOnline&tCategory=trialbyjeory&itemid=WeED01%20Nov%202007%2017%3A36%3A30%3A710

7   http://vids.myspace.com/index.
    cfm?fuseaction=vids.individual&
    VideoID=22311422
8   http://vids.myspace.com/index.
    cfm?fuseaction=vids.individual&
    VideoID=22320819
9   http://vids.myspace.com/index.
    cfm?fuseaction=vids.individual&
    VideoID=22317944
10 http://vids.myspace.com/index.
    cfm?fuseaction=vids.individual&
    VideoID=22310376
11 http://another-green-world.
    blogspot.com/2007/11/two-
    respect-conference-hear-dr-wall.
    html
12 http://vids.myspace.com/index.
    cfm?fuseaction=vids.individual&
    VideoID=22316626
13 http://www.flickr.com/photos/
    eventful/2044110202/in/set-
    72157603225002002/

Standing ovation for Respect's National Chair Linda Smith at the 17 November conference

THE CRISIS IN RESPECT

Chris Harman

Two meetings took place in London on 17 November 2007, in venues about two miles apart. One was the 360-strong annual conference of Respect, which was attended by 270 delegates from 49 local branches and 17 student groups. The other, held in opposition to the conference and under the title "Respect Renewal", was a rally of 210 people called by MP George Galloway and a number of notables, including some members of the outgoing National Council and some of Respect's local councillors.[1]

Such splits are not unknown in the history of the working class movement. The founding of the Second International in 1889 also saw two conferences called in opposition to each other on the same day, in the same city, Paris. One was called by the German Social Democratic Party and the French Marxist party of Paul Lafargue and Jules Guesde, and backed by Frederick Engels, Eleanor Marx and William Morris. The other was called by the French reformist "possibilists" and backed by the British Social Democratic Federation of Henry Hyndman for sectarian reasons. Nonetheless, the divisions in Respect have caused confusion among many on the left in Britain

and are, no doubt, leading to just as great bewilderment internationally. This article attempts to locate the politics behind the division and draw out some lessons.

The eruption of the crisis

Respect's only MP, George Galloway, precipitated the crisis through a series of attacks on the biggest socialist group within the organisation, the Socialist Workers Party (SWP). This began with a veiled attack on Respect's national secretary, John Rees, who is a leading member of the SWP. Galloway also claimed that Respect had wasted resources by sponsoring a 1,000-strong Defend Fighting Unions conference the previous December and by taking part in the Pride London march (one of Europe's largest LGBT rights festivals) in the summer.

By mid-October 2007 the attacks had escalated into an onslaught against the whole SWP. One document circulated by Galloway and his supporters declared, "Respect is in danger of being completely undermined by the leadership of the Socialist Workers Party." The SWP were "Leninists", who were trying to control Respect "by Russian doll methods", claimed Galloway at a Respect branch committee meeting in the east London borough of Tower Hamlets. Local SWP members Paul McGarr and Aysha Ali were "Russian dolls", "members of a group that meets in secret, deciding on a democratic centralist line". Galloway went on to argue, "Paul and Aysha do believe what they are saying" but, he added, "they would have said it even if they didn't believe it".[2] This set the tone for a concerted attempt to drive the SWP out of Respect, with Galloway's supporters unilaterally declaring on 29 October that John Rees was no longer national secretary of Respect and that Lindsey German, the convenor of the Stop the War Coalition, was no longer Respect's candidate for Mayor of London – despite the fact that a 300-strong members' meeting in July had selected her. Five days later Galloway's supporters changed the locks on Respect's national office, shutting out its full time staff. They announced they would not recognise Respect's annual conference and were calling their "Respect Renewal" rally for the same date.

Galloway's supporters tried to justify their moves by making a whole series of groundless allegations against the SWP. They claimed the SWP was trying to fix the outcome of the Respect conference; it was "blocking delegates" in Birmingham; it was voting for delegates "at completely unrepresentative meetings" in Tower Hamlets; it was dragging out meetings in the hope that other people who opposed itwould leave; it was committing the grave sin of urging its members to stand for election as delegates in local branches of Respect; it had made four of the Tower Hamlets councillors "turn their backs on Respect", and was trying to organise a "coup" against the democratically elected leader of the council group and even "trying to do a deal with the Liberal Democrats"; it was claimed that "a fundamental division had occurred in Respect between the leadership of a very small organisation called the Socialist Workers Party and almost everyone else in the party".[3]

The allegations are false, as testified by numerous non-SWP members, including Kumar Murshid, formerly a Labour councillor and advisor to Ken Livingstone, who joined Respect earlier in 2007, and Glyn Robbins, chair of Tower Hamlets Respect. The wording of most of the allegations is remarkably similar to that used by the media against supposed Communists during the Cold War in the 1950s, and by the right in the Labour Party against supposed "Trotskyist infiltrators" in the 1960s and 1980s. The aim was not simply to destroy opposition to a particular direction in which Galloway wanted to pull Respect – a direction that, as we will see, was markedly to the right of the trajectory of Respect when it was launched four years ago. It was also to besmirch the name of the Socialist Workers Party, thereby damaging our capacity to play a part in any united campaign of the left. It was sad to see such methods used by someone like Galloway, who had himself been subject to so much witch-hunting in the past from the media. But tragically he was now engaged in what he described to one activist from a Communist background as a "fight against Trotskyism". No doubt he was more circumspect when recruiting some other people to his side, which includes both Ken Loach and Alan Thornett.[4]

Some such people were, regrettably, taken in by Galloway's lies. But serious activists, however much they might disagree with some of the SWP's politics, know that our members do not behave at all as he purports. Indeed, the SWP has a long record of working over a wide range of issues with people and organisations with different views to our own. Even Peter Hain, now a senior government minister, recalled in a radio programme in October 2007 being able to work with us inside the Anti Nazi League in the late 1970s. He described our party as the dynamic driving force, but said we were able to work with people who were committed to the Labour Party. Today members of the SWP central committee play a leading role in the Stop the War Coalition alongside Labour Party members such as Tony Benn and Jeremy Corbyn, as well as Andrew Murray, a member of the Communist Party of Britain, and people who belong to no party.

Unity and honest argument

There is a reason we have such a reputation. It is because we follow the method of the united front as developed by Lenin and Leon Trotsky in the early 1920s, and further elaborated by Trotsky when faced with the rise of Nazism in the early 1930s. This method stands in direct opposition to manipulating votes or rigging meetings. It starts with the understanding that exploitation, war and racism hurt working people, whether they believe in the efficacy of reform to change the system or believe, like us, that revolution is the only way to end its barbarity. This has two important consequences:

1 Fighting back against particular attacks and horrors depends on the widest possible unity. The revolutionary minority cannot by its own efforts build a big enough movement. Revolutionaries must reach out to political forces that agree with them on particular immediate issues, even if they disagree over the long term solution.

2 By struggling over these issues alongside people who believe in reform, the revolutionary minority can show in practice that its approach is correct, and so win people to its ideas.

It was this understanding that meant that, throughout its history, the Socialist Workers Party and its predecessor, the International Socialists, worked alongside other organisations and individuals – through the Vietnam Solidarity Campaign in the late 1960s, the Anti Nazi League in the late 1970s and the mid-1990s, the Miners Support Committees in 1984-5, and the Stop the War Coalition and Unite Against Fascism today. It was

CHRIS HARMAN: 9 DECEMBER 89

the same approach that led us to initiate a campaign in defence of miners' leader Arthur Scargill in the early 1990s when he was subject to a vicious, lying witch-hunt by the media and the Labour right wing – and most of the rest of the left failed to stand up for him.

Of course, people have attempted to throw mud at us in the past. But the mud has never stuck because we have no interest in manipulation. We cannot fight back without persuading other forces to struggle alongside us, and we cannot win some of those to revolutionary ideas without reasoned argument. Those who have worked in united fronts alongside us know we have always been open about our politics, while simultaneously building unity with those who do not agree with us. To do otherwise would act against both goals of the united front. It would restrict any united front to the minority who are already revolutionaries, making it ineffective. And it would prevent us from being able to show in practice to people who are not revolutionaries that our ideas are better than the various versions of reformism. It would be like cheating at patience.

Anyone with a particular political approach, whether reformist, revolutionary or even anarchist, organises in practice to put across their point of view, even if they sometimes try to deny doing so. And that means getting supporters together, whether formally or informally. Galloway's supporters in Respect could not have issued a stream of emails with between 12 and 19 signatures, and then called a pubic rally in opposition to the Respect conference, if they had not organised to do so as "a group that meets in secret", whether in smoke-filled rooms or through the internet and telephone conversations. As the saying goes, what is sauce for the SWP goose must be sauce for the Galloway gander.[5]

We have always understood that it is necessary to argue for policies that make united fronts effective. So the founding of the Anti Nazi League (ANL) in 1978 involved arguments against those who did not see confronting the Nazis of the National Front as a central priority. A few of the celebrities who initially supported the ANL when it was organising wonderful anti-Nazi carnivals broke with it when the question arose of stopping the Nazis on the streets. If the SWP had not argued with activists across the country, the ANL would never have been able to inflict a devastating defeat on the National Front.

Much the same applied 23 years later when the Stop the War Coalition was formed in the wake of the 9/11 attacks. There had been a highly successful central London meeting, initiated by the SWP and involving others such as George Monbiot, Jeremy Corbyn, Bruce Kent and Tariq Ali. But the first organising meeting after this nearly descended into a disastrous sectarian bun fight as various small groups tried to impose their own particular demands. It was the capacity of the SWP to draw constructive forces together around minimal demands that enabled the coalition to go forward. If some of the sectarian demands had been imposed (such as treating Islamism as if it were as big an enemy as US imperialism) the coalition would have been stillborn. SWP members argued for an approach involving the maximum number of people without diluting in any way its opposition to the war being waged by the US and British governments.

Far from SWP members behaving like "Russian dolls", our capacity to debate what needed to be done within our organisation and then to win others to it was a precondition for creating one of the most effective campaigns in British history. In a previous incarnation Galloway used to praise the SWP for our capacity to get things done, in particular building the anti-war movement of which he soon became a leading member.

The politics of building Respect

The united front method also underlay our approach to Respect. Back in 2003 the anti-war movement was at its highest point. We had seen up to two million people demonstrate on 15 February 2003, as well as a series of demonstrations all over 300,000-strong. Many activists concluded that a political expression for

the movement was required. We shared this general feeling. We also realised that unless a political focus to the left of Labour were built, disillusion could lead, as it had repeatedly in the twentieth century, to an electoral swing to the right – benefiting the Tories and, even worse, Nazi groups. Our duty to the left as a whole was to try to create a credible electoral focus to the left of Labour. We had tried, with only limited success, to achieve this through the Socialist Alliance, which was to a large extent a coalition of existing left organisations (including some that were very sectarian and abstained from the movement against the war). The scale of opposition to the war provided far greater possibilities for building a broad electoral united front.

The left focus would not be a revolutionary one, but would attempt to draw in the diverse forces of the anti-war movement – revolutionaries, of course, but also disillusioned supporters of the Labour left, trade unionists, radical Muslim activists and people from the peace movement. It was a project that only made sense if we could involve large numbers of people who did not agree with us on the question of revolution. To this end, representatives of the SWP leadership were involved in open and frank discussions with various people interested in the same project. Then, the expulsion of George Galloway from the Labour Party precipitated the launch of the project. Again, we followed a united front approach. We agreed on a minimal set of points, fully compatible with our long term goals, which were also the maximum acceptable to our allies, and to many thousands of people drawn into activity by opposition to the war. Hence the name given to the new organisation – "Respect: The Unity Coalition". This was not the full blooded socialist position we might ideally have preferred; if it were it would not have been able to attract all those who wanted some sort of anti-war, anti-racist, anti-neoliberal alternative to New Labour. The initials of Respect summed up the nature of the project – Respect, Equality, Socialism, Peace, Environment, Community and Trade unions – with socialism as one clear point among them.

Once again there was a political fight to get Respect off the ground, and the SWP was essential to this. There was argument inside the SWP, with a few people at a special national party delegate meeting in January 2004 opposing the project or its name. Beyond the SWP there were some on the left who objected to working with Muslims. We had to argue against them, pointing out that Islam, like other religions such as Christianity, has been subject to multiple interpretations – and that the claim that it was innately reactionary was part of the racist ideology being used to justify imperialist wars in Afghanistan and Iraq.

There were also more principled people in favour of working with Muslims, but worried about working with people from organisations influenced by historically right wing versions of Islamism, such as that of the Muslim Brotherhood in Egypt.[6] Against these views we argued that some of those influenced by such organisations were being opened up to new vistas by their involvement in the movement against war, as well as the struggle against Islamophobia, alongside socialists, trade unionists and people of other religious beliefs or none. Only the course of the struggle would show whether particular individuals' horizons had been widened enough for them to be drawn to the left. In any case, as with any united front, what mattered was not chiefly the attitude of the leaders, but whether it was possible to win over their followers, something that would only be discovered in practice.[7] This was important because their following was growing due to the harsh capitalist policies of supposedly secular governments in the Middle East and South Asia on the one hand, and the spread of Islamophobia in Europe on the other.[8]

We also had to argue with people on the left who objected to working with Galloway, claiming his past record ruled this out. He had, for instance, never been a member of the Campaign Group of MPs; he refused to accept that Respect MPs should have a salary no greater than the average wage; he had also attacked the SWP in the past, saying at the time of the 1990 Poll

Tax riot "these lunatics, anarchists and other extremists principally from the Socialist Workers Party were out for a rumble the whole time".[9] But for us, in the summer of 2003, what mattered was not what Galloway might or might not have done in the past, or the level of his salary. The key thing was that he had been expelled from New Labour because he had done more than any other MP to campaign against the war. As such he was a symbol of opposition to New Labour's involvement in Bush's war for very large numbers of people who had previously looked to Labour.

Precisely because the SWP was a coherent national organisation it was able to carry these arguments in a way in which no one else involved in the formation of Respect was. Galloway clearly agreed with this when he enthusiastically agreed to John Rees being nominated as national secretary of Respect, just as Peter Hain and others had once accepted members of the SWP central committee as national organisers of the Anti Nazi League. Hain and Galloway both recognised that a "Leninist" organisation could fight to build unity among people with an array of different political perspectives in a way that a loose group of individuals could not.

We showed our commitment to this over a four-year period. So in the London Assembly and European elections of 2004 we strove to ensure that the Respect lists were much broader than the SWP, even in areas where the SWP members were a large proportion of Respect activists. There were sometimes sharp arguments inside the SWP about making sure non-SWP members were candidates. We recognised this was essential to making Respect into a real "unity coalition". In line with this approach we worked as hard for George Galloway in the 2004 elections to the European parliament as we did for Lindsey German, a leading SWP member who stood for the London Assembly. And we worked as hard in parliamentary by-elections that summer for Muslim convert and journalist Yvonne Ridley in Leicester as we did for John Rees in Birmingham.

It was the willingness of SWP members to work in this way that produced the first electoral breakthrough for Respect in Tower Hamlets when local trade unionist Oliur Rahman became a councillor with 31 percent of the vote. Soon after, SWP member Paul McGarr beat New Labour when he came second in the mainly white Millwall ward in the borough with 27 percent of the vote. No one mentioned "Russian dolls" back then.

In the 2005 general election the diversity of Respect in the east London boroughs of Tower Hamlets and Newham found expression in the candidates for the parliamentary seats in the boroughs. The four -candidates were Lindsey German, George Galloway, Oliur Rahman and Abdul Khaliq Mian. SWP members showed their commitment to Respect as a broad coalition by working for all the candidates, but especially for George Galloway, who was elected as an MP on a Respect ticket. In Birmingham our members worked very hard for Salma Yaqoob.[10] The pattern was repeated in the council elections of 2006. We fought for lists of candidates that were mixed in terms of ethnicity, gender and religious beliefs. In Birmingham, Respect stood five candidates – two Muslim women, a Muslim man, a black woman and a female member of the SWP. In Tower Hamlets and Newham SWP members argued for a mixture of Muslim and non-Muslim candidates in the different wards wherever possible, and others usually accepted our argument. Respect won 26 percent of the vote and three council seats in Newham, 23 percent of the vote and 12 seats in Tower Hamlets and a seat for Salma Yaqoob in Birmingham

Defending Respect as a project for the left

But just as with the Anti Nazi League in the late 1970s and Stop the War Coalition in 2001, the very success of Respect led to political arguments – and SWP members had to try to find ways of dealing with them. One argument flowed from the 2006 election results. The successful candidates were all from a Muslim background, despite Respect winning substantial white working class votes (and a mere couple of hundred votes stopped

non-Muslim candidates winning in Tower Hamlets). This was used by opponents of Respect to spread the idea that it was a "Muslim party".[11]

Another problem flowing from the success of Respect was familiar to people who had been active in the past in the Labour Party, but was completely new to the non-Labour left – opportunist electoral politics began to intrude into Respect.

Problems had already become apparent during Galloway's successful 2005 election campaign in the Bethnal Green & Bow parliamentary constituency. As John Rees writes, there was "a huge alliance aimed at unseating New Labour's Oona King", who was massively unpopular because of her outspoken support for the war on Iraq. But:

Galloway's uncritical promotion of anyone that might get him more votes pulled around the campaign, and promoted within it, individuals and forces very distant from the left. Labour councillor Gulam Mortuza was feted... Local elder Shamsuddin Ahmed was promoted to vice-chair of Respect for his support. Local millionaire restaurateur and property developer Azmal Hussein became a key figure in Tower Hamlets Respect. Abjol Miah, a young member of the Islamic Forum Europe, was celebrated as 'the general' of the campaign. Mohammed Zabadne, a millionaire building contractor, was invited to speak at the victory rally and organised the first victory social a week later.[12]

Socialists did their best to deal with these unhealthy developments. They struggled against the non-left interlopers. By and large the left won. Mortuza turned against Galloway when the left blocked his bid to become "president" of Tower Hamlets Respect, leaving Respect and returning to Labour. Shamsuddin Ahmed was not selected for the council seat he wanted in 2006, left Respect and stood for the Liberal Democrats. Mohammed Zabadne soon became tired of left wing politics and broke with Respect. The willingness of socialists to argue against those who saw Respect simply as a vehicle for their own political careers was vindicated – but, two years later, this was used by Galloway to denounce, by implication, the SWP.[13]

The pressure to shift Respect in a dangerous direction persisted. There is a model of politics increasingly used by the Labour Party in ethnically and religiously mixed inner-city areas – promising favours to people who pose as "community leaders" of particular ethnic or religious groupings if they agree to use their influence to deliver votes. As three local SWP members and Respect activists in Tower Hamlets explain:

The Labour Party held office locally by making deals with, and promises to, key figures in local communities who then delivered "their" votes at election times. Sometimes this was mediated through organisations, religious bodies and individuals which reflected the local population at any time (Jewish, Irish, especially Catholic Irish around the docks, and others). Of course this tradition tended to replace principled politics with, at best, opportunism... With the arrival of Bengalis in east London this old reformist tradition simply adapted itself to the new situation, and has been a central part of Labour's modus operandi in recent decades.[14]

This is what is known in US cities as Tammany Hall politics, or "vote bloc" or "communal" politics when practiced by the - pro-capitalist parties of the Indian subcontinent. It is something the left has always tried to resist. But it was this that began to appear in Respect in Tower Hamlets. There were arguments around this issues in the run-up to the 2006 council elections:

On the selection panel...we were continually being told that "strong" candidates were needed in the most winnable wards. This was a thinly veiled code for selecting Bengali men with a standing in the local area. Of course we recognised that after years of Labour clientalism it was important for the preponderance of candidates in these wards to be ethnic Bengalis. But we also argued that there needed to be a balance across the spread of candidates that reflected all the different elements in Respect's coalition. In order to have a unanimous recommendation from the selection panel we in fact agreed to allow three male Bengali candidates in some wards (all wards had three seats), at the urging of people such as Azmal Hussain and Abjol Miah. Against considerable opposition we did, however, argue that a Bengali woman should stand in Whitechapel, one of our strongest wards, as should John Rees... Despite all of the compromises we made, when the agreed list was put to a members' meeting Abjol strongly objected to John's inclusion in Whitechapel, and although we won the vote we decided to make a tactical retreat from what had been a unanimously agreed position of the selection panel.

It later turned out that two of the Respect councillors, selected on this basis, did not to share the political basis on which Respect had been formed:

One defected to Labour and one resigned. Both felt slighted that their personal ambitions were not being satisfied. Both were Bengali men with some standing in their wards. One was the candidate who replaced John Rees in Whitechapel. Another was, in fact, one of the people hand picked by Abjol and Azmal as the only possible choice in Shadwell.[15]

Arguments also took place in Birmingham in the run-up to the 2007 council elections. The candidate supported by Salma Yaqoob had been in the Conservative Party until just three months before. He had been planning to stand against Respect as an independent in a neighbouring ward. When SWP member Helen Salmon argued against this, Salma Yaqoob said Helen Salmon "had a problem with Asian candidates".[16] Then came the selection meeting for King's Heath – an ethnically and religiously mixed ward. Salma Yaqoob had previously suggested that Helen Salmon should be the candidate. But in the week prior to the selection meeting about 50 people were recruited to Respect in the ward (at a time when there were only about 70 paid-up Respect members in the whole of south Birmingham). An Asian Muslim recruitment consultant was put forward as an alternative candidate at the last minute, and he was selected by 30 votes to 20. The overall outcome of the argument in Birmingham was a complete change in the character of Respect's list of candidates in 2007 compared to the list of year before. There was now a slate made up entirely of men from Pakistani backgrounds.

Typical of the reaction of many local people in Birmingham, Muslim as well as Hindu, Sikh, African Caribbean and white, must have been that of the sister of one Pakistan-born SWP member who said that she had voted Respect previously, but would not do so again because it was a "communalist party".[17] No doubt one of the other parties spread this slander, but events on the ground could be seen as confirming it. Principled socialists had no choice but to argue against such developments. They represented a fundamental shift by sections of Respect away from the minimal agreed principles on which it had been founded – a shift towards putting electability above every other principle, a shift that could only pull Respect to the right. So Socialist Worker ran a short piece criticising what was happening in Birmingham and, a week later, a letter by Salma Yaqoob in response.

Developments in Tower Hamlets also forced principled socialists to take a stand. In the summer of 2006 another bad Labour Party tradition began to come into Respect – the attempt to influence internal decisions by the use of "pocket members" – members paid for and manipulated by individuals within a party. Former left wing Labour councillor Kumar Murshid has explained how this worked on the ground:

One thing that caused me to move away from Labour was the culture of political division and "pocket members" that took hold in the party. You get one or two people with 50 or 100 pocket members who come into political meetings to decide positions or nominations. They grab power without any support in real terms – and the politics just gets thrown out the window.[18]

Balwinder Rana argues that the same methods have been used by the Labour Party in Southall, West London: "When an election is coming up, they go door to door, getting membership and paying their membership dues from their own pockets".[19] Now

attempts were made to use similar methods at Tower Hamlets Respect members' meetings. One wealthy member turned up with dozens of membership applications and a wad of money to sign people up at the reduced rate for the unemployed so they could vote at a meeting to decide who would head the Respect group on Tower Hamlets council.

Arguments also took place within the newly elected Respect group on the council. Four councillors, including Respect's first elected councillor, trade unionist Oliur Rahman, and its two women councillors, objected to what they saw as right wing positions taken by the majority of the group, and the failure of this majority to use their positions to agitate and campaign for Respect's positions. None of the objectors were at that point in the SWP, although two soon joined. The issues became sharper late in the summer of 2007 when one of the Respect councillors resigned his seat in Shadwell, triggering a by-election. A Respect selection meeting got heated when a young woman, Sultana Begum, dared to stand against a middle aged man, Harun Miah. The SWP members and the four left wing councillors decided that Sultana Begum had the sort of fighting spirit best suited to represent Respect. Making this choice was one of the alleged "crimes" of the SWP referred to by Galloway – even though SWP members, after losing the vote at the selection meeting, worked flat out to win the seat for

Respect, and were even thanked by the successful candidate.

Our real "crime", it seems, was that we argued out politics openly and vigorously, and refused to be dragooned into being "Russian dolls" for George Galloway's friends.

The mystery of Galloway's turn

For some, the mystery in this account may be why Galloway turned so suddenly against the SWP. We can only surmise what his motive might have been. But his record is clear. He behaved marvellously immediately after his election by going to the US Senate and denouncing the war in front of the world's television cameras. But after that his role rapidly became rather different to that of the "tribune of the oppressed". There were complaints that he tended to leave much of his constituency work in Tower Hamlets to those whose salaries he paid out of his MP's allowances.

Then, at the beginning of 2007, he dealt a blow to everyone who was preparing to campaign for Respect in the local elections: he absented himself from politics for weeks to appear in the despicable "reality TV" show Celebrity Big Brother. Every active supporter of Respect was faced at work with taunts from the right and with people on the left saying they would never vote for Respect again. The SWP had to decide how to react to this. The pressure was particularly acute during these weeks because leading Respect members such as Ken Loach and Salma Yaqoob were keen to denounce Galloway. Fortunately, as a "Leninist" organisation of "Russian dolls" we had our annual conference just as Celebrity Big Brother started and were able to agree on a general reaction, which our members then tried to argue. We pointed out that appearing on the TV progamme was stupid and an insult to those who had worked to get him elected, but that it was not in the same league as dropping bombs to kill thousands of people in Iraq and Afghanistan. We defended Galloway at meetings of the Respect leadership, in an article putting the case in Socialist Worker and through statements on television by John Rees and others. We never, of course, got any thanks from Galloway for this.

It is probably fair to say that, had SWP had not defended Galloway during the Big Brother affair, Respect would have disintegrated at that stage. Nevertheless, there is no doubt that the Big Brother farce hit our vote that May. Galloway never once acknowledged the damage he did. On the contrary, in the months after the fiasco he began to use his "celebrity" to build a career as a radio talkshow host, interspersed with television appearances and, again insulting to Respect activists, appearing as guest presenter on the Big Brother's Big Mouth in June 2007. Yet he had the gall just two months later to complain that the SWP was "undermining" Respect. Meanwhile he had achieved the dubious record of being the fifth highest earning MP, after the former ministers William Hague, David Blunkett, and Ann Widdecombe, and the Tory columnist and candidate for Mayor of London, Boris Johnson. Some tribune of the people!

Despite his increasing preoccupation with his media career throughout most of 2006 and the first half of 2007, Galloway was still capable of letting us have occasional glimpses of his old skills at denouncing imperialism. He remained an asset to the left, even if a diminishing one, and we in the SWP reacted accordingly. We never imagined he would suddenly attack us for resisting those who were pushing sections of Respect in the direction of electoral opportunism. So we continued to try to get him to speak on Respect platforms, even if media commitments limited his availability, and we defended him against a further attempted witch-hunt.

When he suddenly did launch his attack with the document of mid-August, anyone capable of looking a little below the surface could see it was directed against us. The document appeared when New Labour unexpectedly began to hint there might be a general election within four or five weeks. Galloway had said he would not stand for reelection to his seat in Bethnal Green & Bow, but he did show a desire to stand in the other Tower Hamlets constituency. That required him to win votes. So his document was based, in part, on

electoral arguments. Respect had done poorly in the Ealing & Southall parliamentary by-election. For those with a modicum of political analysis, this could be explained by the timing (it was called at two and half weeks notice), by the fact that it was in the middle of the short-lived "Brown bounce" as the new prime minister came into office and by our lack of roots in the area. But Galloway contrasted it with the success of Respect in the Shadwell ward by-election in Tower Hamlets, drawing the conclusion that the only way to win seats was to follow the methods which had begun to take root in parts of Birmingham and Tower Hamlets. There was no future in appealing to workers on the basis of class or anti-war arguments (despite the victories of SWP members Michael Lavallette and Ray Holmes in council elections in May) and instead there had to be a shift towards courting "community leaders". The SWP was resisting such a turn, and so it had to be attacked.

Breaking points

The attack on the SWP was centred on the area where Galloway and his ally Abjol Miah hoped to be Respect parliamentary candidates, Tower Hamlets. There was an explosive meeting in mid-October to elect delegates to the annual conference. The question of "pocket members" raised its head again. Scores of people attended who activists had never seen before. As Kumar Murshid wrote in a letter to one of Galloway's supporters, Azmal Hussain, who chaired the meeting:

The fact that you and your colleagues mobilised so many members to come to the meeting yesterday was fantastic, except that most everyone I spoke to did not really know why they were there or what they wanted. I put to you that this is precisely the problem when your energies are given to the pursuit of positions and supposed power as opposed to political issues around which we need to define ourselves and our party.

The Respect rules stipulated that nominations for delegates had to be received in advance of the meeting. In all, 46 nominations had been received and there were a number of vacant places. An account by SWP members tells what happened next:

Just before the vote was about to be taken Kevin Ovenden [paid parliamentary assistant to Galloway] brought in a second handwritten list. This list contained names of people who were not fully paid up members of Respect, people who had not been asked if they wished to stand, people identified by only one name and one member of Newham Respect who was proposed from "George's office". After the chair, Azmal Hussain, refused to put a compromise proposal to the vote the meeting became chaotic and the chair and a number of others left. Jackie Turner, Tower Hamlets Respect secretary, took over in the chair with the agreement of the meeting

and the original nominations were ratified and it was agreed to discuss with the proposers of the second list how the remaining places could be filled.[20]

George Galloway, who was not at the meeting, put his name to a denunciatory email claiming the SWP had "systematically undermined" the meeting, ignoring democratic procedures so as to take control of the conference delegation.[21] When the SWP and the left councillors defended themselves, he accused us of aggression. At the "Russian dolls" meeting in Tower Hamlets he told some of our members (including his 2005 -election agent) to "fuck off". Some of his supporters made it clear they wanted to drive us out of Respect. They attempted to do so at another Tower Hamlets meeting the following week. But seeing that they did not have clear majority Azmal Hussain, in the chair, refused to take any votes against or abstentions on their resolution and then tried to end the meeting when people objected.

One very disturbing feature of this meeting was the attitude of Galloway's supporters towards women members of Respect. Rania Khan, at 25 the youngest councillor, recalls:

We had about 50 women that night and they had valid membership cards but they were not allowed to take part. It was raining and cold outside and they had small children with them, and someone who was close to the council group leaders said to one of the women queuing up outside, "My wife doesn't come, why are you here?"[22]

This was not the first time such attitudes had been displayed towards to Respect members, and particularly young women. Lufta Begum says that Respect council group leader Abjol Miah "shouted at me". Paul McGarr says, "Some of the young Muslim women have been repeatedly insulted and bullied." He adds that he does not see this as a particular characteristic of Muslim men – it was how women would have been treated by Labour officials in the mining village he grew up in 40 years ago. The point, however, is that the left have always sought to resist such behaviour.

Up to this point the SWP had done its utmost to reach a compromise that would prevent the split in Respect coming out into the open. Our only precondition was that principled socialists had to have the right to argue within Respect's democratic structures against opportunism and Tammany Hall communalism. But the behaviour of Galloway and his supporters in Tower Hamlets showed that compromise would not work. There was only one possible way of keeping Respect alive in its original form – for the SWP and others on the left to fight flat out. The left councillors were so angry by this point that no one could dissuade them from breaking with the rest of the Respect group on Tower Hamlets council. As Lufta Begum says, "John Rees said to us,

don't resign the whip at present. But we could not endure it any more".

Resigning the whip did not, as Galloway's supporters claimed, mean them leaving Respect. There is a long tradition in British politics of elected representatives losing or rejecting the "whip" (ie the discipline of the parliamentary or council group) of a party without leaving the party itself.

The internal discussion in the SWP

Galloway and his supporters have portrayed the SWP as a closed "Leninist" group in which a small number of people at the centre dictate to the members, who then are frogmarched into manipulating wider meetings. The picture does not correspond to the way the SWP really works. This was shown by the way we reacted to the attacks on us from late August onwards.

Once it became clear just how serious Galloway's attacks were we circulated his first document and our reply to our members, and called a meeting for all London members. The meeting was chaired by an experienced member, who had argued for an alternative slate for the central committee to the one proposed by the outgoing leadership at the 2006 party conference. There was open debate, with alternate speeches from those who supported and those who opposed the central committee's   interpretation   of events. And there was not the slightest hint of intimidation, with a strict ban on heckling. A series of members' meetings in each locality followed and then a national delegate meeting. Again, those who disagreed with the leadership's position were able to speak without hindrance – including three non-delegates who were invited as the only observers so they could make their points. At the end of the meeting a vote was taken in support of the leadership's reply to Galloway's arguments and it was carried overwhelmingly in a room containing more than 200 people; there were only two "noes" and four abstentions. Arguments on both sides in the debate within the party were then printed in an internal bulletin; all the arguments within Respect were circulated to party members; further local aggregate meetings took place and then another national meeting, attended by about 250 people, which voted with two against and a handful of abstentions to endorse a central committee document.

One particularly sad thing in this whole sorry saga was the behaviour of three SWP members, who had every right to put their arguments to the party, and had done so at the meeting of London members, in the party's internal bulletin and at the first national delegate meeting. Two of these members, who had both been in the party for a number of years, had taken employment as Galloway's assistants. They chose to ignore the overwhelming feeling

at the SWP's national meeting and not only lined up with him, but also helped orchestrate the attacks on the SWP and the left councillors in Tower Hamlets. The third, a former member of the Militant organisation, was asked by the central committee not to stand for the position of national organiser of Respect, but insisted on putting himself forwards for this job. We had no choice but to part company with the three and terminate their membership of the SWP. The vote at the second national meeting held by the SWP endorsed this decision.

No one reading the account of the succession of meetings and discussions we organised should be able to conclude that our "Leninism" or "Trotskyism" is undemocratic. Thousands of people with a record of activity in the working class, anti-war and anti-racist movements had access to all the different arguments and followed them attentively before coming to a conclusion. They decided overwhelmingly that they would not be "Russian dolls" for Galloway as he tried to turn Respect into a vehicle for furthering the political careers of people who shared few of its original values.

The conclusion of our discussions was that it was necessary to try to continue to build Respect according to the original conception as a left focus reflecting the diversity of the forces involved in the anti-war movement. This could only be done by opposing the attempts by Galloway and his allies to stifle accountability of elected representatives, to prevent Respect members from challenging moves towards opportunism and to drive the biggest group of organised socialists from positions of influence in Respect. To this end, every effort had to be made to ensure that the Respect annual conference took place with delegates elected on a democratic basis. It was while we were deciding on this approach that news came through that Galloway's supporters were trying to sabotage the conference by calling their own rally on the same day. Galloway's rally consisted to a very large extent of speeches denouncing the SWP.

Results and prospects

Respect has not been the only attempt to build a left alternative to a right moving social democratic party. We have seen similar attempts with the Scottish Socialist Party, P-Sol in Brazil, the Red-Green Alliance in Denmark, the Left Bloc in Portugal, Die Linke in Germany, the efforts to find a single anti-neoliberal candidate for the presidential elections in France in 2007 and the formation of Rifondazione Comunista in Italy. Neither has Respect been the only case in which the project has suddenly been endangered by the behaviour of leading figures.

The Rifondazione leadership in Italy moved very quickly from intransigent opposition to the centre-left to joining a centre-left government implementing the

policies it once opposed. The majority of the leadership of the Scottish Socialist Party gave evidence in a libel trial against the party's best-known figure, Tommy Sheridan. The Portuguese Left Bloc was thrown into disarray in the autumn of 2007 by the decision of José Sá Fernandes, a left wing independent activist elected to Lisbon council with the Bloc's support, to make a deal with the Socialist Party. The Red-Green Alliance in Denmark was paralysed in the run-up to the November 2007 elections by a media campaign directed against the organisation's decision to choose a young Muslim woman as one of its main parliamentary candidates. There are continuing tensions inside the German Die Linke over the participation of some of its East German members in local government coalitions with the social democrats. The attempt to put forward a single presidential candidate for the anti-neoliberal left in France, backed by nearly half of the Ligue Communiste Révolutionnaire (LCR), came to nought. The French Communist Party claimed its own candidate represented the movement, while José Bové, himself claiming to be the "unity candidate", attacked the Communist Party and the LCR, only to agree later to be adviser on "food sovereignty" to the right wing Socialist Party candidate Ségolène Royal.

None of this means that the attempt to create a left focus is in itself misplaced. The meagreness of the reforms offered by Labour and other social democratic parties has created a huge political vacuum to their left, which the forces of the revolutionary left are too weak to fill more than partially by themselves. It is this which creates the need for a gathering of left forces wider than the revolutionary left organised through a united front. But the very thing that makes such political united fronts potentially able to attract wide support – the involvement of well known -non-revolutionary political or trade union figures – necessarily means they are unlikely to last indefinitely in the face of changing circumstances without intense arguments breaking out over their direction. Figures who believe in the path of reform rather than revolution can often put up very strong and principled opposition to what a particular government is doing at a particular point in time. But their very commitment to path of reform means that they can suddenly drop some of their principles in favour of opportunistic attempts to advance within the existing structures of society.

Galloway, for instance, has been open about his commitment to the path of reform. He has said that the Labour government would have been very different "if John Smith were still alive". On television and radio programmes he has often demonstrated a strange faith in the capacity of the police to deal with crime, and has declared his commitment to the unity of British state, which he sees New Labour as undermining.

Such views meant that at some point he was likely to be attracted to opportunistic methods that revolutionary socialists would have to resist. The same was true of Bové in France, of Sá Fernandes in Portugal and of Rifondazione's leader Fausto Bertinotti in Italy. It also cannot be ruled out in the case of the most important West German leader of Die Linke, Oskar Lafontaine. This does not mean it has necessarily been wrong to form a political united front with such figures. However, it requires an awareness that the very success of such a project can embolden reformist as well as revolutionary forces, encouraging them to go off in their own direction and to attack viciously those who resist.

The point was made in this journal three years ago that "electoral splits from an existing mainstream reformist party necessarily involve activists who reject the policies of current governments, but who have not broken with the whole conception of parliamentary socialism". This would inevitably mean "when the going gets tough there is pressure among activists whose political background has been in mainstream reformism to fall back on the methods of parliamentary alliances". It was necessary for revolutionaries to go through "the experience of trying to build an alternative with people who are still at least half influenced by reformist ideas – but also do not hide their distinct views and take every opportunity to win people to them through their publications, their meetings and one to one arguments".

The assumption then was that the "pressure" towards opportunism would arise when there were openings for supposed influence at the governmental level, as with Rifondazione in Italy and previously with the Alliance Party in New Zealand. What was unexpected was the much lower level of temptation required for prominent figures to break with declared principles. The examples of the Scottish Socialist Party, of Buffet and Bové in France, and of Galloway should have taught us all a hard lesson.

This does not, however, mean that the method of the political united front is wrong. It is likely to continue to be essential in the period ahead as the way to channel the bitterness against social democrats abandoning the interests of their traditional supports. But it is necessary always to remember any particular configuration may be of limited duration, with some forces turning their back on it even as new ones open up fresh possibilities.

This also means it is wrong to conceive of the left focus taking the form of a "broad party", united over the whole range of policies, rather than a coming together in of a coalition of independent political forces and traditions – some revolutionary, some reformist. There is no way that reformists and revolutionaries can agree on all their political objectives without

dishonesty and manipulation on one side or on both. The LCR in France has a different attitude to the role of working class in the struggle to change society to that of Bové or Buffet. George Galloway and the "community leaders" in Tower Hamlets or Birmingham have a quite different attitude to those of us who are consistent revolutionaries. Unity to fight mainstream parties is one thing. An agreed programme on how to change society is another.

These arguments also apply in important forms of day to day activity. In Britain trade union leaders sympathetic to Respect agree with revolutionaries on opposition to anti-union laws, but they may well be opposed to urging particular groups of workers to take unofficial action in defiance of them. In Germany, union leaders who support Die Linke have not agreed with the correct decision of some Die Linke branches to back a strike by an independent train drivers' union.

Where revolutionaries are very few in number, their options for united action may be restricted to working in a much bigger organisation where left reformism predominates, while being able to do little more than make propaganda for their own views within it. But where the revolutionary and reformist forces are more evenly balanced, revolutionaries have a duty to argue and agitate independently, even as they work with others in the political united front. This has one very important practical implication.

It means a revolutionary press that does not restrict its arguments to those shared by its reformist allies. Only in this way can it provide a coherent Marxist view of the world and not fudge over what needs to be done in each concrete, immediate struggle.

These lessons are going to continue to be important. The few dozen people who think of themselves as revolutionaries but have joined the Respect Renewal breakaway will learn this lesson the hard way. They will face a choice between having to avoid speaking on a whole range of issues or saying things that upset one or other of its component parts. They will be faced on a daily basis by Galloway, with his disdain for what ordinary supporters think about his media performance and his opinions of issues such as crime, by those Tower Hamlets councillors whose main concern is their own careers, by those who mistakenly believe the only way to win the votes of Muslim workers is to keep quiet in the face of male chauvinist attitudes, and those who despite their denials have tried to play the communal card in the past and will do so again in future. We can only hope that at some stage principle wins in the battle with opportunism.

Meanwhile, the main body of Respect faces the continued challenge of trying to build a consistent left focus. That will be harder after the breakaway. But wider political developments are likely to offer new opportunities in the medium term. The crisis in Respect arose, in part, because the immense feeling against the war was not matched by a corresponding increase in the level of industrial struggle, allowing union leaders to use their influence to endorse New Labour. And the crisis came to a head in the late summer because the "Brown bounce", however short-lived, worried those whose only concern was short term electoral success. But New Labour is now facing renewed problems as Gordon Brown reveals his true face, not only through his commitment to Bush's wars in Iraq and Afghanistan and threats against Iran, but also through his attempt to hold down public sector wage rises below inflation, and his continuation of Blairite policies in education and the health service. The breakaway of the Galloway group from Respect may have been a blow to the attempt to provide a left focus for those disillusioned by New Labour. But revulsion at Brown's policies should provide plenty of opportunities to recover from it.

END NOTES
1   Respect Renewal claim a much higher figure, but 210 was the maximum number of people allowed in their hall under fire regulations, and is confirmed by counting the numbers present in photos posted on websites.
2   Transcript of the emergency meeting of Tower Hamlets Respect branch committee, Thursday 18 October 2007. From

notes taken down by Maggie
Falshaw.

3   The first four of these allegations
    were contained in the stream
    of emails sent by Galloway's
    supporters to Respect members;
    the last two were in a letter
    published in the East London
    Advertiser, signed by the leader
    of the Tower Hamlets councillors'
    group, Abjol Miah, and Galloway's
    two full time assistants Kevin
    Ovenden and Rob Hoveman.

4   Alan Thornett is the leader of
    the British section of the Fourth
    International.

5   This is especially so since
    some of Galloway's allies in the
    Islamic Forum of Europe have
    connections with the Bangladeshi
    group Jamaat-i-Islami. Founded
    in pre-Independence India, this
    group developed as a very tight
    knit politico-religious organisation
    in both West and East Pakistan.
    It was involved in the military
    suppression of the Bengali
    liberation movement in 1969,
    before developing separate
    Pakistani and Bangladeshi wings,
    both of which still use force to
    drive the left from university
    campuses. Until recently the
    Bangladeshi Jamaat was in
    government with the right wing
    National Party, while the Pakistani
    Jamaat has been part of the
    alliance that has governed in
    coalition with General Musharraf's
    supporters in one province.

6   This was, for instance, the position
    of Tariq Ali and Gilbert Achcar

7   For the general argument, see
    Harman, 2002.

8   This was the tone of my
    arguments in fraternal debates
    with Gilbert Achcar at the SWP's
    Marxism festival in July 2005
    and at the Historical Materialism
    conference in December 2006.

9   Quoted in Morley, 2007, p201.

10 For the character of the Respect
    election campaign, see Taylor,
    2005.

11 The interviews in Taylor, 2005,
    give a very different picture.

12 John Rees, "Respect: Anatomy
    of a Crisis", SWP Preconference
    Bulletin 3 (December 2007).

13 Galloway complained of
    "tensions" caused at one Respect
    meeting to select council
    candidates in his document
    "The Best of Times, the Worst
    of Times", which triggered the
    crisis.

14 Shaun Doherty, Paul McGarr
    and John McLoughlin in SWP
    Preconference Bulletin 2
    (November 2007).

15 Shaun Doherty, Paul McGarr
    and John McLoughlin in SWP
    Preconference Bulletin 2
    (November 2007).

16 Helen Salmon, Pete Jackson
    and others, SWP Preconference
    Bulletin 2 (November 2007).

17 Information provided by Talat
    Ahmed.

18 Interview in Socialist Worker, 17
    November 2007.

19 Speech at Respect conference.

20 Shaun Doherty, Paul McGarr
    and John McLoughlin, SWP
    Preconference Bulletin 2
    (November 2007).

21 Email to members of Tower
    Hamlets Respect by Azmal

Hussain, George Galloway and others, 16 October 2007.

22 Interview with Rania Khan, 17 November 2007.

23 Speech at Respect conference.

24 Speech at Respect conference.

25 This article is based on that document. I have changed some of the wording to make sense to a wider audience than SWP members and I have put in additional material dealing with events since the meetings. The original document is available of the SWP website: www.swp.org.uk

26 As the bitterness of Galloway's attacks on the SWP increased we argued that working for him was becoming incompatible with loyalty to other SWP members. They rejected the suggestion and were clearly on Galloway's side at National Council meetings of Respect and local meetings in Tower Hamlets. Their abandonment of the SWP was proved when they rejected the offer to appeal to the party's disputes committee against the central committee's decision to expel them.

27 Trudell, 2007.

28 Gonzalez, 2006.

29 This is what he said on one occasion in the presence of Colin Barker. John Smith was the leader of the Labour Party in the early 1990s after Neil Kinnock and before Tony Blair.

30 Question Time, on BBC 1, 25 October 2007, available on George Galloway's website.

31 Harman, 2004.

REFERENCES

Gonzalez, Mike, 2006, "The Split in the Scottish Socialist Party", International Socialism 112 (autumn 2006), www.isj.org.uk/index.php4?id=247

Harman, Chris, 2002, The Prophet and the Proletariat, second edition (Bookmarks).

Harman, Chris, 2004, "Spontaneity, Strategy and Politics", International Socialism 104 (autumn 2004), www.isj.org.uk/index.php4?id=12

Morley, David, 2007, Gorgeous George: The Life and Adventures of George Galloway (Politico's).

Taylor, Ian, 2005, "Respect: the view from below", International Socialism 108 (autumn 2005), www.isj.org.uk/index.php4?id=137

Trudell, Megan, 2007, "Rifondazione Votes for War", International Socialism 113, (winter 2007), www.isj.org.uk/index.php4?id=284

THE SWP TAKES A STEP BACKWARDS

Cllr Salma Yaqoob

Of all the words written about the split in Respect, the least important are those dealing with who did what at some meeting or other. Of much more interest are those articles attempting to provide some political explanation of these events.

Two recent articles from Martin Smith and Chris Harman[1] attempt to provide this political explanation. What I propose to do here is to address three aspects of this debate. Firstly, the SWP's echoing of attacks once the preserve of those more known for pandering to Islamaphobia than challenging it. Secondly, the SWP's crass understanding of the dynamic of race and class inside the Muslim community, and the conclusions they draw from it. And thirdly, how best to protect the political integrity of the newly emerging Respect as an entity rooted in opposition to war, neo-liberalism and racism.

A spectre is haunting Respect?

Leading members of the SWP are conjuring up the spectre of reactionary religious forces on the march inside Respect.

In his article in the December 2007 issue of Socialist Review, SWP National Secretary Martin Smith quotes, with apparent approval, an opponent of Respect as saying: 'The split will strengthen the weight of the Islamists in Respect Renewal, some of whom have links to Jamaat-e-Islami [Pakistan's largest religious party]. I don't think that's going to make the party very hospitable to socialists.'[2]

Chris Harman echoes the theme, but goes for a double whammy, invoking two apparently sinister organized forces at work inside Respect: '...some of Galloway's allies in the Islamic Forum of Europe have connections with the Bangladeshi group Jamaat-i-Islami...It was involved in the military suppression of the Bengali liberation movement in 1969, before developing separate Pakistani and Bangladeshi wings, both of which still use force to drive the left from university campuses'[3]

This argument could not be clearer: conservative Islamic organisations are organizing inside Respect against socialists. It is an argument that we have heard time and time again from those who most viciously opposed Respect from the start, as part of their pro-war agenda. That the SWP now echo these arguments is astonishing.

To ascertain whether there are conservative Islamic religious forces exercising their weight inside Respect, it is first helpful to evaluate whether they are emerging in broader British society.

Writing about this nearly two years ago my estimation about Muslim radicalism, - those engaging in political activism from a self consciously religious perspective - was as follows:

'...the dominant character of Muslim radicalisation in Britain today points not towards terrorism or religious extremism, but in the opposite direction: towards political engagement in new, radical and progressive coalitions that seek to unite Muslim with non-Muslim in parliamentary and extra-parliamentary strategies to effect change...the existence of this new and progressive radicalism is a sharp break from those who would lead British Islam into confrontation with all levels of British society.'[4]

As evidence I pointed to increasing Muslim participation in an array of campaigns and initiatives, from the anti-war movement to the European Social Forum, from political alliances with the Mayor of London's office to the emergence of Respect.

Two years later that process has deepened. The decision of the MCB to end their boycott of Holocaust Memorial Day[5], the comments from its chair Mohammed Bari that discrimination on the basis of sexual preference was 'obnoxious',[6] and the growing relationship between the MCB and the Trades Union Congress represents important progress. Reactionary and conservative religious radicals certainly exist, and their influence has to be continually countered. But the general political trajectory of Muslim radicalism is still towards progressive politics.

That general trend is much more dramatically pronounced inside Respect, which has gathered together a significant grouping of Muslims who combine their Islamic faith with a commitment to the struggle for social justice.

One indication of which way the wind is blowing has been the complete absence of any serious dissent inside Respect over the kind of secular/religious fault lines that run through wider society. This includes issues such as abortion law, homosexuality, gender equality or faith-based schools.

For many people these are matters of personal morality and religious belief. For that reason we would be wise to deal with them with some sensitivity[7]. But these issues, of course, have a wider political and social significance that we cannot ignore. In this context, an argument about the importance of the right to self-determination, freedom and equality is very powerful. I have argued on many occasions that if Muslims demand respect for their beliefs and lifestyle, then the same tolerance and respect for the rights and choices of others is obligatory.

What we have achieved is the creation of an alliance which emphasizes universal themes of justice and equality. Within this there will be all sorts of ideological (and theological) views. But they are united by the defence of the rights and freedoms of all. It is an alliance that has advanced support for progressive social causes.

There is no evidence of any Muslim bloc inside Respect seeking to give our political agenda some Sharia flavour. There is no evidence that members of Jamaat-i-Islami or any other Islamic organization are on some 'entryist' mission inside Respect.

There is no evidence of the SWP raising concerns about undue religious influence in all the time I have been Vice Chair. And there is no evidence that such forces are about to emerge in the absence of the SWP. Quite the opposite, in fact. When we were organizing the Respect Renewal conference the Islamic figure our Bengali councillors in Tower Hamlets wanted to speak was Tariq Ramadan, the most progressive exponent of a modern European Islam.

The SWP allegations are groundless. They are driven more by the dynamic of a faction fight in which they are grasping around for ideological cover to mask what is in reality sectarian manoeuvres to entrench their control. The danger for the SWP, in repeating arguments which first emanated from the so-called pro-war 'left', is that in so doing they allow the waters of Islamaphobia to lap at their feet.

Are Muslims in retreat from the struggle against war and racism?

The SWP have suggested that there is a retreat from engagement in radical politics by Muslims, and that George Galloway was adapting to this reversion to conservative community politics. They locate

this retreat in the impact of the 7/7 bombings. This claim is wrong.

There is no evidence that Muslims, radicalised by the impact of war and Islamaphobia, are falling in behind Home Office attempts to incorporate establishment figures on the basis of softening opposition to British foreign policy or to their campaigns of demonisation against Muslims. The handful of Muslim figures who have taken such a view patently do not have the support of the wider community. Any political benefits the Labour party have gained from the 'Brown Bounce' have very much disappeared. While there is fear and concern over new government threats to our civil liberties, there is simply no evidence that the Government's agenda is substantially weakening the anti-imperialist or anti-racist consciousness among any significant layer of Muslims in Britain today.

The SWP attempts to justify this argument with reference to a decline in the numbers of Muslims attending anti-war marches. This is far too simplistic. The inability of the anti-war movement to prevent the invasion of Iraq inevitably had a certain demoralizing effect, across all communities, undermining a belief in the power of social movements to make a difference. It was not just Muslim participation on anti-war protests that subsequently declined.

But the anger over the war on terror has not gone away. It re-emerged over the Israeli attack on Lebanon, and would undoubtedly emerge again in the advent of any new escalation like an attack on Iran. Furthermore, events organised by coalitions of Islamic institutions such as the Global Peace and Unity conference and Islam Expo have continued to grow after 7/7 and have continued to develop a critical, radical edge. These attract tens of thousands of participants.

It is a mistake therefore to conflate a dip in Muslim involvement in a single set form of activity – a Stop the War demonstration – with a major political regression to community politics.

Does Respect pander to 'community leaders' i.e. small businessmen'[8]?

Related to this mistaken analysis, is a crude understanding of the appeal of Respect inside the Muslim community. The SWP states: 'This logic of electoralism has led Galloway and his supporters to be drawn into making alliances across the whole Muslim community', wherein, George Galloway, myself and others will become increasingly dependant upon 'community leaders' i.e. small businessmen'.[8]

It is true that Respect does have an appeal across the whole Muslim community. There are two possible explanations for this. One, traditionally favoured by the ultra-left and now by the SWP, is that Respect has consciously courted the support of community leaders/small businessmen, at the price of politically compromising ourselves. Again, no actual evidence is produced to substantiate this, nor is there any explanation as to why

sections of the Muslim business community would think their class interests are best served by hitching their wagon to a fringe political party.

Another explanation lies in an understanding of how racism impacts on all Muslims. This racism affects all Muslims, although of course it is mitigated by class background.

Firstly, though, one must be clear about the nature of Muslim communities in Britain today. Muslim communities are dominated by disadvantage and poverty[9].

• Around 69% of Muslims live in poverty.

• 35% of Muslim households have no adult in employment – double the national average. Overall, they are 3 times more likely to be unemployed than the population as a whole.

• 73% of Pakistani and Bangladeshi children live in households below the poverty line – compared to 31% for all households

• 32% of Muslim households were overcrowded, and generally Muslims have poorer housing conditions, and are more reliant on social housing

• 28% of young Muslims are unemployed

• 20% of Muslims are self-employed – frequently in marginal and insecure occupations

These are the communities where we have won our strongest support – in some of the poorest wards in the country. Our support does not come primarily from the small, or not so small businessmen, seeking to advance their interests. It comes overwhelmingly from those who experience poverty and disadvantage.

But, in tandem with this poverty and disadvantage, is racism. Irrespective of their class background, Muslims are constantly aware of the discrimination and prejudice they face. It is no less real for the self-employed taxi driver, or the owner of a small grocers shop. There is anger throughout the community at this racism, compounded by anger at the blatant double standards of Western foreign policy.

A consequence of this system of disadvantage and exclusion is the pitifully poor political representation imposed on these communities. For many years this has been dominated by the Labour Party, happy to rely on the large votes from Muslims, but desperate to retain control over them.

So when politicians come along who articulate the feelings of the community, they will get respect, whether they are Muslim or non-Muslim. One of the biggest reasons why Muslims say they support me is that I make them feel proud of who they are, even to the extent of thinking I am a role model for their children.

This sense of pride and community loyalty applies to Muslims who are unemployed, it applies to Muslims who run corner shops, and it applies to our handful of more wealthy backers.

There are Muslim businesspeople who live in million pound mansions in leafy suburbs, while operating businesses in our communities paying low wages and delivering poor conditions for their workers. But I have not yet found these people to be natural supporters of a fringe left-wing party. There are other businesspeople who both live and work in our communities, and who retain a close connection with the community they come from, and who have the same interest as their brothers and sisters in confronting racism, opposing war, and seeing good representation for the disadvantaged areas they live in.

Respect's base is among the poorest sections of our communities. And the experience of anti-Muslim racism, and disgust at imperialist war, motivates some small business people in those communities to join us. The roots of our cross community support do not lie in right-wing, anti-working class politics. They can be found in a commitment to oppose racism and war, and the significance of a political party being seen to speak out in defence of that community's interest.

Running through the SWP's analysis is a crude reductionist attempt to read off all political actions from some supposed economic interest. If this is too simplistic in trying to explain Respect's support from some people who own small businesses, it is even more so in relation to people seen as community leaders. The single biggest reason such individuals acquire weight and influence is not wealth, it is reputation.

South Asian communities are built on the basis on migration. New immigrants settle where they have already family or personal links. As a result, most of Birmingham and Tower Hamlets Muslim communities live in areas with others of a similar background. That background invariably lies in common village roots in Pakistan, Kashmir and Bangladesh, with ties reinforced through marriage. These strong community ties bring real benefits. They have provided an indispensable leg-up to newly arrived immigrants from rural areas as they navigate their way around their new country.

The value of such support is incalculable, and is not readily forgotten. And on the basis of their records in doing such work, certain individuals can acquire prestige and influence. It is insulting to our voters and supporters to reduce the prestige which certain individuals in the community have, to some form of patronage or favour they dispense.

Of course this influence can be, and often is, abused. Family and clan loyalties have allowed influential figures in the community to claim control over blocks of votes that can run into the hundreds. This system can stifle genuine political debate, and at its worst can lead to corruption of the electoral process.

But the existence of such loyalties is a reality that cannot be wished away. Family or clan loyalties are not an invention of 'community leaders'. They originate in the social structures of India, Pakistan and Bangladesh, and persist because of the experience of migration and the importance of mutual support and interdependence in the daily lives of South Asian communities in Britain today.

This social reality can be both a strength and a weakness. And it leads to real pressures which we have to resist by asserting the primacy of principled politics.

Our campaigns to end the postal vote have to be seen in this context. It is for the reasons that biraderi (extended clan) networks can exert undue influence that we have been campaigning vigorously in Birmingham against postal votes. Women in particular have been disenfranchised. Postal votes are filled out in the "privacy" of one's own home. But it is not private when family members, candidates or supporters, can influence - subtly or otherwise - the way you complete your vote. Community leaders may claim to be able to yield significant voter blocs, but no one can interfere with the secrecy of the polling station. A secret ballot means that loyalties to family and friends can be maintained in public, but political arguments can still win out in the real privacy of the voting booth.

Ultimately, however, we have to stick to principles and lead by example. Last year in Birmingham Sparkbrook we came under considerable pressure when we selected a candidate whose family were originally from the same village in Pakistan as the sitting Lib Dem councillor. It was alleged we were splitting the biraderi vote. And that we could not win by so doing. We resisted those pressures, just as we resisted pressures when the same people said we could never win by standing a women candidate. And we were proved right on both occasions.

The SWP's allegations that we are in thrall to 'community leaders i.e. small businessmen' are as ignorant of the communities they profess to be knowledgeable about as they are misleading about the actual activities of their critics.

Respect: the politics of 'Tammnay Hall' and 'pocket members'?

The SWP claim that following the outcome of selection meetings in Birmingham and Tower Hamlets the character of Respect changed, and there was a move 'away from the minimal agreed principles... towards putting electability above every other principle'.[10] They also claim that 'Tammany Hall' politics i.e. the buying of ethnic voter blocs in return for political favours, have now corrupted Respect.

These are about as serious a set of allegations as can be made.[11] You would expect therefore that the SWP to produce evidence to substantiate them. You would expect them to be able to point to how the political programme

of Respect has been subsequently watered down; or to cite examples of our elected councillors pandering to a pro-war, neo-liberal agenda; or to give a single instance where our councillors have abused their elected positions or brought Respect into disrepute. Yet no evidence is forthcoming.

The SWP's attempt to evoke an analogy between Respect and the practices of the Democratic Party machine - known as Tammany Hall - is particularly ludicrous. For decades, Tammany Hall politics played a major part in controlling politics and carving out ethnic voter bases in cities like New York City and Chicago through patronage, bribery, kickbacks. It was first and foremost based on the use and abuse of power – a real power which, by any definition, is lacking among Muslim communities in Britain.

There is no parallel between the Tammany Hall system and the attempts by disadvantaged and excluded minority communities in Britain to organize themselves to exert influence over the political system. The former is a colonial-type operation to keep politics in the hands of big business. The latter is a struggle for justice and equality by those kept out of the corridors of power. One would have thought the SWP could tell the difference between the two.

All sorts of groupings organise to maximize their influence in society. I see no reason – other than ignorance and prejudice – why the organization of minority communities should be singled out for particular hostility, particularly when representatives of those communities do not wield significant political power in our society.

Of course, pressures exist and have to be countered. We have seen allegations, over many years, of 'pocket members' bought and paid for by individuals with the sole intention of influencing selection meetings.

These undemocratic practices can be dealt with. Membership rules can be tightened, or in extreme cases a national party can intervene if a local organization is bringing it into disrepute. Prior to the split I am not aware of the SWP either proposing new measures to tighten membership requirements or raising at a national level their concerns about selection processes inside Respect.[12]

Instead they overplay the outcome of a few selection meetings where their preferred candidates did not get selected. There is more than a touch of double standards here. The SWP complain about candidates encouraging their supporters to 'pack' a meeting.[13] Yet the SWP goes through the same process every time it approaches a contentious meeting or conference. It will have its full-timers ensuring that the membership details of its supporters are up to date - no doubt in some cases using SWP district bank accounts to speed the process. And when their side wins, they congratulate themselves on

a 'good mobilisation'. When the other side wins, they cry foul about meetings being 'packed'!

The SWP, with a half a century of political existence behind them, came into Respect as a well-organised party, with an apparatus staffed by fulltimers and an extremely top down and centralised decision making culture. With a familiarity of operating in committees and party political structures that the vast majority of Respect's new supporters and members did not have, the potential for an organised political grouping having an influence wholly disproportionate to its social base among Respect voters, was very real.

As it became clear that Respect's strongest voter base and elected representatives came from within sections of the Muslim community, where the SWP had virtually no influence, so they increasingly resorted to bureaucratic manoeuvrings and control to exercise influence. By packing a committee with their members, by acting in committee meetings to a prepared plan and in a disciplined manner, they could lockdown the decision making structures in their favour. New Respect activists learnt the only way to challenge this was to outplay the SWP at their own game, and 'pack' meetings better than they could, which they duly did.

Whichever side 'wins' in these sort of contests, it has to be admitted that the process brings with it an unhealthy dynamic into our internal life. The coalition model that Respect was founded upon had its merits. In the future, however, I am convinced that we need to organise much more along traditional party political lines. We need to be clear that we are building a political party, and not making some form of temporary agreement between rival interests for electoral purposes.

Conclusion

I see nothing that has happened in the last year or so that fundamentally challenges my view that the political foundation upon which Respect rests – opposition to imperialism, neo-liberalism or racism – is anything other than solid.

Those in the leadership of the Renewal wing of Respect are implacable on all these three fundamental issues. Likewise, the bulk of our members and supporters have essentially old Labour values, given backbone with anger at war and racism. Our members feel pride when they hear Respect leaders like George Galloway articulate their concerns with his trademark eloquence and uncompromising anti-imperialism and anti-racism.

Many come from backgrounds in the South Asian sub-continent where they are all too familiar with the reality of political corruption; and certainly in inner city Birmingham, they will have seen similar practices replicate themselves in the behaviour of

the Labour Party. By contrast they see us as embodying political principle.

This is what our reputation rests on. But we can't take it for granted. We have to work hard to protect it.

We must create a more rounded and extensive political culture so that our members absorb through a variety of means our fundamental principles, and where new leaders and candidates are moulded out of our traditions. That is a process. It will require determination and consistency on our part. To that end the production of a Respect newspaper is one important step in the right direction. More steps will follow. However I am confident of the political direction we are travelling. I am also confident that Respect is emerging reborn and renewed from its recent difficulties.

NOTES AND REFERENCES

1   Martin Smith, 'Where next for Respect?' Socialist Review December 2007
    Chris Harman, 'The Crisis in Respect', document sent to IST members, December 2007.
2   Smith opt cit.
3   Harman opt cit.
4   A point George Galloway repeated in his letter to the SWP concerning their attempt to brow beat Muslim councillors into participating on a Gay Pride float.
5   Salma Yaqoob, 'British Islamic

Radicalism' in Islamic Political Radicalism: A European Perspective, editors Raymond Tallis &, Tahir Abbas, Edinburgh University Press, 2006

6 http://www.muslimnews.co.uk/paper/index.php?article=3299

7 http://www.tuc.org.uk/the_tuc/tuc-13179-f0.cfm

8 John Molyneux, 'On Respect: a reply to some points', SWP pre conference discussion bulletin 3, 2007.

9 http://www.nya.org.uk/Templates/internal.asp?NodeID=92837

10 Harman opt cit.

11 For somebody who allegedly prides himself as a practitioner of a scientific Marxist method, the paucity, anecdotal and one-sided nature of Chris Harman's evidence is striking. The fact that in order to substantiate his claims about Birmingham Respect he is reduced to reproducing a comment from a friend's sister, who apparently happens to live in Birmingham, and who allegedly thinks Birmingham Respect is 'communalist', has more than a touch of desperation about it. Nobody that I know has ever heard of the source he quotes; for all I know she might not even be a Respect member. And if she is, she is certainly not an active one. It is revealing he can't find any members from his own organization active in Birmingham Respect to publicly reiterate and substantiate the 'communalist' charge. They certainly have never made any such charge at any Respect meeting that I have attended. The only other piece of evidence Harman produces in relation to Birmingham is a disputed selection meeting held last year. He cites the fact we selected seven Asian males as evidence of succumbing to conservative patriarchal pressures from inside the Muslim community. He conveniently ignores the fact that the most high profile Respect figure in the city is a Muslim woman. He also ignores any reference to my request to the SWP that they come forward with female candidates for the outstanding 33 uncontested wards: http://www.socialistworker.co.uk/art.php?id=10628 The bigger question SWP members should be asking themselves about the Kings Heath selection meeting is why, in a catchment area that included Birmingham University and a 6,000 plus student population, the SWP could not recruit even half a dozen of so students to support their candidate, Helen Salmon.

12 The SWP proposed changes to membership only after they had elected to 'go nuclear' over George Galloway's letter, and Respect was in the process of dividing into two. Their proposal was that members should be restricted as to how many members any individual member could recruit

in any one month, that the
National Office should be able
to ask prospective members
for proof of their right to the
concessionary rate, and that
new members had to attend a
minimum number of meetings
prior to voting for candidates
etc.

The first of these proposals
was clearly unenforceable,
but also bizarre in its demand
that members should limit
their recruitment aspirations.
Respect's problem has not been
too many members but too few.
The second proposal promised a
potentially racially inflammatory
test of the veracity of members.
Bangladeshi members in Tower
Hamlets have already had plenty
of experience of condescending
white members demanding ID
from them as though they were
having to pass an immigration
entry test. The third and most
significant restriction however
was clearly an opportunist device
to keep control over selection
of candidates and election of
officers in the hands of those
for whom attendance at political
meetings was a way of life – this
likely to be, of course, mostly
SWP members. So much, then,
for trying to create a new kind of
organisation which would help to
enfranchise those who had for
so long been disenfranchised.
Most extraordinary of all,
these proposals also promised
restrictions which are not to be
found in either the Labour Party
or the trade union movement.

The SWP proposals threatened
to entrench the tendencies,
marked in many areas, of making
Respect an extension of the
local SWP branch's campaigning
activity rather than giving it a life
of its own.

13 Rob Hoveman adds the following
background information in
relation to Tower Hamlets:
"In four years in Tower Hamlets,
in the area where we have the
biggest support for Respect
electorally and where we have
had an MP for almost three
years, an examination of the
membership of Respect in the
borough revealed that the SWP
had recruited virtually no-one
white to Respect outside the
SWP itself. This represents an
abysmal failure. Moreover,
according to their local
organizer, a Tower Hamlets SWP
branch meeting was told that
60% of the SWP members in the
borough had not joined Respect
and that they would, in the face
of the "witch-hunt" the party
was facing, now be trying to get
them to join!

"Much has been made about the
process of candidate selection
in Tower Hamlets for the council
elections in 2006. What was most
apparent in the run-up to the
local elections, however, was, on
the one hand, the lack of white
candidates to put up for election
and, on the other, the fact that
the SWP candidates, most of
whom were white, had had no
real prior connection with or
involvement in the Bangladeshi

community which was inevitably going to be the major source of votes in the election.

"Few, if any, of the SWP candidates in Tower Hamlets had serious roots in the wards in which they stood. Of no-one was this more true than John Rees. Although he had worked in the area for many years, as this was the site of the SWP national office until the last couple of years, he had not been involved in local campaigns and in fact lived in Hackney.

"He wanted to stand in Whitechapel because this is where he though he was most likely to get elected. A number of Bangladeshi activists thought this unlikely as no-one in the Bangladeshi community in Whitechapel had any prior knowledge of him. This was the one source of acute division at the candidate selection meeting in the Kingsley Hall, where the room divided almost but not exclusively on racial lines over his standing in Whitechapel. Although his candidacy was confirmed at that meeting by majority vote, he subsequently concluded that he could not win there and switched to Bethnal Green South as a more promising prospect. Even so he did not really start his local campaign until four weeks before the election and concentrated heavily on getting SWP members in to canvas by knocking on doors.

"I was in favour of John Rees standing in the election but the tactics deployed to try to get him elected seem to me to have been fatally flawed. Throwing in wave after wave of canvassers in the last few weeks, when most psephologists will tell you most votes have already been decided, shows an incredible lack of understanding about how confidence, and therefore votes, are won amongst sections of the community. And hoping to ride the coat-tails of Bangladeshi candidates who do have roots and the connections betrays an electoral opportunism (unsuccessful in this as in other cases) entirely counter to the long-standing SWP position that SWP members need to build real roots in the community.

"Finally, in relation to SWP claims about there being something underhand about new members being recruited before the candidate selection for Bethnal Green and Bow in November 2007, what they did not point out was that many of the new members who were being registered were being registered by SWP councillor Lutfa Begum in order to vote for her daughter Rania Khan to be the candidate. Rania Khan incidentally was the SWP's own preferred candidate for the nomination. There may well be nothing improper in Lutfa Begum encouraging new members to join in the run-up to a selection. But what is improper is the SWP's double standards when it comes to such actions."

A REPLY TO CHRIS HARMAN

Alan Thornett

Chris Harman claims that his article *The Crisis in Respect* is an attempt to locate the politics behind crisis in Respect. It is nothing of the sort. It is a continuation of the method the Socialist Workers' Party (SWP) has employed in the debate around the issue from the outset, which has been to bury the politics behind an ever-increasing welter of allegations and distortions mostly, but not only, about George Galloway and Salma Yaqoob.

To the extent that he does deal with the politics it is an attempt to defend the indefensible i.e. the 'loose coalition' model of organisation which the SWP insisted on for Respect and the way the SWP leadership reacted to George Galloway's letter at the end of last August.

Harman claims that the crisis was precipitated by a series of attacks on the SWP. It was not. It was precipitated by the astonishing over-reaction of the SWP leadership to George Galloway's letter, which called for some rather modest changes in the way Respect was organised and run. The letter did not imply a crisis or a split in Respect. It did, it is true, add up to a critique of the SWP and the way it ran Respect. But it was impossible

to criticise any aspect of Respect without this being the case, since the SWP were running it from top to bottom. Respect was, in effect, by then, a wholly-owned subsidiary of the SWP. That was in fact the nub of the problem the letter was trying to address.

Harman also claims that the letter was designed to shift Respect to the right. It was not. There was absolutely nothing in the letter to suggest such a shift. The issues Harman singles out in an attempt to establish this are the questioning (in the context of financial administration) of the decision to spend £2,000 on the hiring of an expensive float for the 2007 Gay Pride at a time when Respect had no money, and the resources put into the Organising Fighting Unions conference (OFU) and the subsequent £5,000 loss. There can be different views on these issues but they were both legitimate questions to raise and neither of them held any water at all as examples of a move to the right.

In fact Lesbian, Gay, Bisexual and Transgender (LGBT) rights are an unfortunate subject for Harman to pick to attack the letter, given the SWP's dubious record on the subject inside Respect. There have indeed been clashes with George Galloway over this issue in Respect. Whilst Galloway supports LGBT rights, and has a record of doing so, he has controversially argued on several occasions for the issue to be given a lower profile in Respect material. The problem for

Harman, however, is that the SWP have, on each occasion, supported Galloway over such proposals against Socialist Resistance (SR) supporters, and others, who have argued for a higher profile.

This was the case at the first two conferences of Respect, where SR supporters were denounced by SWP leaders for raising resolutions highlighting LGBT rights. It was also the case with the first draft of the Respect manifesto, which I wrote, where George Galloway was also supported by SWP leaders when he argued for reducing the profile of this issue. Whether it was right or wrong to suddenly spend a lot of money on an intervention into the 2007 Gay Pride parade, when previously SR supporters had to campaign to get a leaflet produced for Pride, can be discussed. But it was not a shift to the right. It was what it was: the questioning of particular expenditure at a time when Respect had no money for an election campaign or anything else.

There was always a legitimate question to be asked about the way the OFU conference was built and resourced through the Respect office and full-time staff. I was opposed to the way it was built from the start, and declined to be a part of the organising committee as a result. I had argued for a conference organised jointly with sections of the trade union left, and if possible with the Communist Party of Britain (CPB), with the aim of strengthening the links between Respect and the trade union left and other partners in the project.

This approach was rejected on the Respect officers' committee in favour of a conference called and organised by Respect itself – with the main aim of getting the maximum attendance. In the event, the conference. although quite big. did nothing whatsoever to strengthen the relationship between Respect and the trade union left. It was perfectly legitimate for George Galloway to criticise the resources put in by the Respect office, and the £5,000 loss incurred.

Gay Pride and OFU, however, were side issues in the Galloway letter. In any case, Harman himself argues elsewhere in his article that the shift to the right is an intention behind the letter, rather than in the text of the letter itself. What Harman fails to take up is the central issue of the Galloway letter: the state that Respect was in. The stark reality was that the membership of Respect had declined from 5,500 two years earlier, to 2,200 by August 2007: something which would normally be seen as a crisis. Not only were many of Respect's branches moribund or inactive, but Respect was politically narrower, since the bulk of those who had left had been independent activists. It had financial problems and it was in no position to face a general election. There were problems with its decision making process, the functioning of its elected committees, and the undemocratic top-down control exercised by the SWP. These were the real issues which provoked the letter.

None of these were new problems. Some of us had been raising them for several years. The Respect Party Platform (RPP) – had tried to raise them at the Respect conference in October 2006 and had been roundly slapped down by John Rees (Respect National Secretary and a leading SWP member), with the support at that time of George Galloway. The declining membership was blatantly covered up. In fact, falsified membership figures were presented to the conference by John Rees. These were designed to give the impression that Respect had grown when it had declined. All protests about this manipulation were ignored.

The conference was told that, in any case, membership figures were not the best way to measure the strength of Respect: that there were a lot of Respect supporters who were not prepared to join, but could be called upon in important campaigns like elections. This was an oblique – but revealing – reference to SWP members and the way the SWP saw Respect. This was that it did not need to be a real organisation, with real members, because there were plenty of SWP members who could be drafted in as foot-soldiers as necessary. It meant that Respect was not a real organisation at all but a front for the SWP! It did not have any internal political life of its own because it did not need an internal life. It was an extension of the SWP: a device to be used at election time. SWP member after SWP member went to the rostrum to denounce us and to claim that their Respect branch was vibrant and expanding, that there was no crisis and that it was malicious to suggest otherwise. The following is an extract from the RPP assessment of the conference, published soon after:

"The real situation inside Respect was the elephant in the room which must not be mentioned. How, following major electoral gains winning a seat in Westminster and then 16 councillors in the local elections was Respect smaller and politically narrower at the time of the conference than at any time since it was founded despite the gains in East London.

"According to the annual report, as discussed at the National Council prior to the conference, Respect had lost a third of its members over the past year, down from just over three thousand to just over two thousand, and many of its branches are in bad shape. Yet far from using the conference to discuss this problem and how to tackle it, the whole thing was covered up. The version of the annual report given to the delegates had even been altered, and all the membership figures removed. A carefully worded formula was inserted in place of the figures which gave the impression that the membership had gone up. It was smoke and mirrors. A declining Respect becomes an expanding one. George Galloway in his opening speech not only claimed that everything in the garden was absolutely rosy but that Respect had just recruited

10,000 students! Respect was, said Galloway 'the fastest growing party in Britain'. John Rees insisted that Respect was 'bigger this year than last year'."

All proposals we put forward at the conference to address this disastrous situation were also slapped down by an SWP majority. The implication was that since there was no crisis – other than in the heads of a disgruntled minority – there was no need for any solutions either. We were successfully isolated and defeated.

This was the real background to George Galloway's letter. What was new was that they had now been reflected in a poor result in the Southall Parliamentary by-election, there was a general election in the offing, and George Galloway had now raised them. The letter was an attempt to tackle this situation. It made proposals for a much-needed membership and fund drive and a modest reorganisation of the leadership structures of Respect, to bring a bit of plurality in at the top. If the SWP had been prepared to discuss the issues politically and make some compromises, to show that they were prepared to take other people's views into account, there could have been a positive outcome. John Lister (the other SR member on the Respect NC) and I issued a statement welcoming George Galloway's letter as far as it went, but calling on him to go further, particularly over the democratisation of Respect internal procedures and structures, and on accountability.

Harman says rather patronisingly that those from the left like me, John Lister (and Ken Loach and others) who supported the letter and eventually supported Respect Renewal were confused! But there was never any doubt where we would stand on the letter. It was pointing to problems we had been raising and changes we had been proposing for a long time. Nor was there any chance from the outset that we would support the SWP leadership once it was clear that they were opposing the letter in favour of an unacceptable status-quo. If the fiction of a left/right divide was calculated to draw us into the SWP camp, it was never going to work.

This was the reaction of almost all the non-SWP members of the NC. It was a remarkable situation. The SWP leadership managed to alienate themselves, within a few weeks, from virtually all of the active non-SWP members of the NC: people they had been working with for three and a half years. There were 50 members of the NC, of which about 44 were actively involved. At the time of the letter, the SWP had 19 members of the NC. By the time of the split, 19 NC members supported Respect Renewal and 21 supported the SWP, of which 17 were SWP members (several others declined to take sides).

Among those supporting Respect Renewal are Linda Smith (the National Chair of Respect and leading member of the Fire Brigades Union), Salma Yaqoob

(National Vice-Chair and elected councillor in Birmingham), Victoria Brittain (a well known writer and playwright), Jerry Hicks (leading industrial militant and member of the SWP at the start of this crisis). There was also film maker Ken Loach, Abjol Miah (the leader of Respect on Tower Hamlets Council), Yvonne Ridley (also a journalist), and Nick Wrack – the first national chair of Respect and a member of the SWP when the crisis broke.

One feature of the SWP Respect after the split is that the ratio of SWP members to independent activists on its National Council elected on October 9th is even greater. SWP members are seventy percent of the incoming NC. It will be difficult to have much of a coalition on that basis.

Harman claims that the SWP did its "utmost" to reach a compromise to prevent a split. It did not. In fact it was the SWP's total refusal to compromise which set a split dynamic in train. Far from making concessions, the SWP went totally in the opposite direction. They took the letter as a frontal attack on the SWP and launched a nation-wide tour of SWP districts vilifying George Galloway and scandalously calling him and Salma Yaqoob (amongst many other things) "communalists", with its divisive connotations for those from the Sub-Continent, of brutal colonial pogroms and imperialist divide and rule. They also characterised his letter as a part of a right wing attack on the left in Respect.

The charge of communalism was particularly outrageous in the case of Salma Yaqoob, who, far from being a communalist, had a high profile and exemplary record in combating it in Birmingham – which she convincingly outlined in her reply to the SWP Challenges for Respect.

There may well have been examples where Respect focussed too much on building in one single community or worked too much through community networks in a particular area. The SWP are seriously wrong, however, in describing this as communalism and Harman continues with this dangerous line. Of course, the task is to resist relying on such networks and especially where, which is often the case, they are male-dominated. Unlike The Labour Party, however, we need to fight for transparent processes, as has been the case over postal voting. If there have been concessions to these practices, the SWP have to show what they did about it at the time not just claim, without any evidence, that it was all down to George Galloway. Salma Yaqoob covers some of these things a lot more adequately in her excellent reply to Harman – A Spectre is Haunting Respect?

At each of the SWP's internal meetings the attacks on George Galloway became more frenzied. A minority which emerged inside the SWP in opposition to all this, and which argued for the SWP to make compromises before it was too late, was brushed aside and some were later expelled. In hindsight, is it probable that once the SWP leadership had gone down the road of whipping up their members against Galloway in this way, it was already impossible to prevent a split. It was very difficult to pull back from the kind of allegations which were being made and the bitterness engendered. So SWP leaders, finding themselves in a hole, kept digging. In fact, the kind of language used then continues in Harman's letter. In it he not only claims that there was a witch hunt against the SWP, but that it reflected the tone of the Cold War of the 1950s and the purges of Trotskyists in the Labour Party in the 1980s! At another point it compares us with the leadership of Rifondazione joining the Prodi coalition.

It is worth noting that the George Galloway the SWP were now vilifying was the same George Galloway that the SWP had repeatedly shielded from criticism from ourselves and others ever since Respect was founded: not just on the profile of LGBT rights, but other issues as well. They now denounced him for unaccountability, yet at the time of the Celebrity Big Brother debacle they fought might and main to protect him against any degree of accountability at all. They successfully blocked any of criticism of his decision to go on the programme being expressed by Respect. Harman repeats the crassest arguments deployed by the SWP at the time to defend their

actions. For example: that George Galloway's appearance on Big Brother was not as bad as invading Iraq as Blair and new Labour had done! So that's alright then! On that criterion he had a completely free hand!

Harman's answer to the charge that the SWP undemocratically dominated Respect – something which was so recognisable to non-SWP members – is to claim that it cannot be true because the SWP has a good reputation in campaigns such as the Anti-Nazi League and the Stop the War Coalition! Whether this claim holds water or not his answer reflects the scale of the problem. The SWP has indeed always treated Respect as a single issue campaign and sought to build it as such. This is the infamous united front of a special kind – when it needs to be something much more akin to a political party if it is to succeed. The level of democracy, of involvement of members, and of common political experience and development, is something very different in an organisation (whether you call it a party or not) which fights for political office than in a single issue campaign which is confined to a limited objective. Again this was the nub of the issue.

Harman claims that George Galloway and others have attacked democratic centralism and Leninist organisation. What has been challenged, however, it not democratic centralism as such, but the way the SWP operated democratic centralism inside Respect, and the effect this had on the democracy of the organisation. In other words, the SWP's bureaucratic conception of 'democratic' centralism and the way they applied it to Respect. The objection was not that the SWP had meetings as the SWP. The objection was the relationship between its decision making processes and those of Respect itself. Many in Respect, who were not in the SWP, were becoming painfully aware as to what this involved. It meant the huge SWP delegations on the leading bodies of Respect acting under democratic centralist discipline as normal practice, with no attempt to limit the impact of this, or allow a genuine process of discussion to take place. This made it a waste of time for others to attend, since all the important decisions were determined in advance. I had declined nomination for the officers group (the executive committee) after the 2006 conference for exactly this reason, because my attendance was pointless. The elected committees were not the real decision-making bodies at all. They were token meetings controlled by the parallel decision-making structures of the SWP. Decisions which were taken were only carried out if they corresponded to the SWP agenda.

It was this dubious mode of operation which required a top-down structure with the 'important leader' at the top running both Respect and the SWP. And it was this which was challenged by George Galloway's proposal to establish a national organiser alongside the national secretary, with equal authority. This also explains why this proposal was resisted so strongly by the SWP. It was seen as a direct challenge to John Rees and his ability to run things this way.

It was this issue rather than events in Tower Hamlets in East London which was the driving force of the split on the NC. After several hours of debate at two NC meetings – during which SWP delegates came close to driving George Galloway out of Respect – an agreement was reached on the appointment of a national organiser with equal status to John Rees. It was seen as a breakthrough by the non-SWP members of the NC. An officer's meeting then set this decision aside and referred the issue to the Respect conference. That decision took the crisis to a new level. It sent a message loud and clear that the SWP was going to defend their top-down conception to the bitter end, and that it was probably too late to save Respect in its original form. It was also this which brought the crisis in Tower Hamlets to a head and triggered a battle over conference delegates. If everything was going to be decided by a vote-out at conference, delegates became crucial.

There had been wider problems and conflicts in Tower Hamlets Respect, it is true. Many of them reflected genuine problems arising out of Respect's electoral success, however, for which nobody should apologise. Respect made a major breakthrough – unprecedented on the left – into impoverished working class minority communities in East London and Birmingham, amongst people who were outraged by the war. A large number of new members, many of whom had little experience of the labour movement or the traditional left, with different traditions of political organisation, came into Respect. But how those gains could be consolidated and built, and how the problems which would inevitably arise could be tackled (whatever new community was involved) was another matter.

It is true that Respect's appeal as an anti-war party had an impact right across the Muslim communities in a way which would not be the case in a white working class area, for example. There were – and are – restaurant owners who strongly support Respect again in a way that would not be the case in a white working class area. But this is a product of the position such people find themselves as migrants in British society, their political experience back home, and the nature of the so-called war against terror with its demonisation of Muslim people.

It would be a big mistake, however, to conclude that the several restaurant owners who support Respect Renewal determine the class character of that support. They absolutely do not. The bulk of Respect's Muslim supporters are amongst the most

impoverished sections of the working class in Britain. It casts shame on the SWP that they are now resorting to arguments which previously came either from the right wing or the ultra left.

The problems arising from all this, of course, were never discussed in Respect at the level of the NC or the even the officers group. Harman makes a series of allegations about Tower Hamlets Respect about non-left interlopers and the like. But why was none of this brought to the elected committees at the time? The fact is a conscious decision was taken by SWP leaders to keep them internal to Tower Hamlets and the SWP, since the elected bodies were not seen as the real leadership. That was the SWP. Instead of collective discussion, the problems, where they existed, were internalised and compounded. It was a big mistake. It was impossible for the elected leadership to take responsibility for such problems when they were not informed of the existence of them. Instead of discussion and debate around issues as they have arisen, the SWP's answer was lowest-common-denominator politics. It avoided conflict but nothing was resolved.

The political framework behind all this was the 'loose coalition' conception – which the SWP had insisted on imposing on Respect – rather than building it as an all-round political party. With a loose coalition, the priorities were not political development and the establishment of collective political experience. These were seen as the preserve of the SWP itself, which is a logical approach with a united front campaign. For such a campaign or a loose coalition, the priority was to be able to be able to deliver votes when they were needed. How the organisation itself developed was a secondary matter.

There were also implications for internal democracy. A loose coalition does not imply the same level of democracy or accountability as a party. Nor does it imply the detailed rules needed for standing for political office, policy making, membership status, selection procedures and accountability. Harman alleges irregularities in Tower Hamlets, specifically of large numbers of members joining at the unemployed rate – when some of them, he argues, must have been employed. It is hard to know whether there was substance in this allegation or not. But what is clear is that the SWP has an appalling record of overlooking such irregularities when it has suited them. This raises questions as to how such a situation, if it existed, was allowed to develop in the first place. Both the 2006 Respect conference and the SWP-organised 2007 Respect conference featured large numbers of student delegates who had no legitimate status at all. They were 'elected' from the lists of students who simply expressed an interest in Respect at a Freshers' Fair, but never joined, and in most cases were never seen again. It was one of the factors making

the conference an undemocratic and unacceptable event which was no longer viable as a united conference. It would have been unlikely ever to get past the item 'endorsement of delegates' then breaking up, which would have done no one any good.

Harman makes no serious attempt to explain the SWP's dramatic switch – as far as George Galloway is concerned – from unquestioned leader to number one enemy of the left. It's true that Galloway is a maverick and is a controversial politician. But he was both of these things the day Respect was formed and he remained so the day it split. At the time Respect was formed, the SWP saw it as important to include someone like Galloway in a project like Respect, if it was to have a broad appeal. And they were right, at least in principle, even if they got it wrong in practice. You can't have a broad party including both revolutionary socialists and left reformists without any left reformists of any weight and influence. And Galloway is still the only left Labour MP to make a break with Labour, having been expelled from Labour over the war – and to have put his weight behind building an alternative. He is the best public speaker on the left, not an unimportant attribute, and was and remains a central leader of the anti-war movement. It is largely from these two factors that he has the biggest electoral base of anyone on the left outside of the Labour Party. He is left

Labour in his politics, as he made very clear at the Respect Renewal conference. But it was this which he brought into Respect from the outset – a genuine component of left-Labour politics.

Nor is Harman right to draw a parallel between the Big Brother episode and Galloway's other media appearances – in particular his twice weekly Talk Sport show. This is a left-wing show and is a service to the left. It is used by GG to promote left-wing causes and left-wing ideas in front of an audience of half a million. It is hard to see and objection to that.

The degree of success achieved by Respect Renewal since the split is both an indication that the political conditions for such a party remain as strong as ever. Respect Renewal remains fragile and will only develop successfully to the extent that it is able to turn outwards towards the rest of the left. The strength of Respect Renewal, however – which was never the case with the original Respect under the SWP – is that it is serious about approaching other sections of the left, such as the trade union left and the CPB, about a wider regroupment of forces to tackle the crisis of working class representation. It is serious when it says that it does not see itself as the answer, but only one component of the answer. It means it when it says that if it is possible to move towards a wider regroupment, it would put no organisational preconditions in the way. Its only precondition would be that it would represent a step forwards in building the kind of new party the working class needs in order to respond to the betrayals of social democracy.

All these issues could have been discussed in the framework of the old Respect had the SWP leadership acted differently. Unfortunately, that was not the case. In reality, there was resistance to this kind of approach. The task now, therefore, is to make Respect Renewal the success it has the possibility of being. It has made a very encouraging start; the task now is to build on this initial success.

RESPECT NEWSPAPER

One of the first actions of Respect Renewal following the split recorded in these documents, was the rapid production of Respect's first genuine newspaper.

Produced over the two weeks following the 17 November Respect Renewal conference, it includes articles on ecology and global warming, a 2-page spread on Palestine, and reports on the campaigns to defend trade union activists Karen Reissmann and Michael Gavan.

The paper has been produced partly with resources offered by Socialist Resistance, which announced at the 17 November conference that it would cease production of its own paper Socialist Resistance in order to give full support to the new Respect publication

OUT NOW!

FIRST ISSUE OF RESPECT'S MONTHLY NEWSPAPER

■ Peace ■ Justice ■ Equality ■

Respect

A monthly newspaper — No. 1 December 2007. 80p

Palestine pages 10-11

Brown's bluster won't halt climate change

Phil Thornhill, organiser of the Campaign against Climate Change

In 2001 when Bush rejected the Kyoto protocol it didn't make the front page of the Guardian. Now climate change seems to pop up on the front pages all the time. Now everyone knows it's an issue.

So as campaigners on this issue since 2005 can we say we're getting somewhere at last?

● *More on climate change and debate on contraction and convergence – see inside pages 12-15*

In fact emissions of greenhouse gases since 2007 have skyrocketed globally – even here in the UK CO2 emissions have risen, not fallen. But our failure is not just measured in such statistics. It's frighten-

ingly apparent all around us as Greece and California burn, as the Amazon dries out, as the arctic ice shrinks to 60% of what it should be. Anybody who has cast an even fairly dispassionate eye on the science knows we are engaged in a desperate race against time.

In these circumstances increased awareness is not enough – not unless it's channelled in such a way as to result in effective action, real and rapid reductions in emissions. That why the kind of awareness, the sort of messages that are out there, matters.

What we have so much of is TV adverts telling you to switch off the lights, posters in the tube telling you not to boil too much water in your kettle, a thousand websites telling you how to reduce your 'carbon footprint'. As if by all living purer more carbon-free lives we could solve the problem.

Why as in theory we could, but we all know it just isn't going to work that way. The reality is that only a minority will be doing these things, so at best the process will be deeply unjust because a carbon-serious minority will be carrying the can for a don't-care majority.

But in fact the total amount of carbon saved by all these good intentions remains, in the grand scheme of things, negligible – it could be easily wiped out by one bad investment decision made by government.

Just about everything that can be done by individual effort can be done better and more fairly by government regulation.

Continued inside, p 12

Did you know?

■ In India and Bangladesh, over 700 people lost their lives this summer due to flooding and mudslides (not counting those who subsequently died of water-borne diseases.)

■ The Canadian Arctic Survey recorded temperatures of 22 degrees this summer: that's 15 degrees above the long term average.

Brown's credibility collapses into farce

Between a Rock and a police inquiry

page 3

Catastrophe in Bangladesh

East London responds to cyclone disaster

page 15

Nurse's vital fight against victimisation

Defend Karen Reissmann!

page 7

INSIDE: ● Home News ● Trade Unions ● International News ● Debate ● Councillors ● George Galloway MP

RESPECT'S 14-POINT PROGRAMME

- An end to the war and occupation in Iraq. We will not join any further imperialist wars.
- An end to all privatisation and the bringing back into democratic public ownership of the railways and other public services.
- An education system that is not dependent on the ability to pay, that is comprehensive and gives an equal chance in life to every child no matter how wealthy or poor their parents, from nursery to university.
- A publicly owned and funded, democratically controlled NHS, free to all users.
- Pensions that are linked to average earnings.
- Raising the minimum wage to the European Union Decency threshold of £7.40 an hour.
- Tax the rich to fund welfare and to close the growing gap between the poor and the wealthy few.
- The repeal of the Tory anti-union laws.
- Opposition to all forms of discrimination based on race, gender, ethnicity, religious beliefs (or lack of them), sexual orientation, disabilities, national origin or citizenship.
- The right to self-determination of every individual in relation to their religious (or non-religious) beliefs, as well as sexual choices.
- The defence of the rights of refugees and asylum seekers. Opposition to the European Union's 'Fortress Europe' policies.
- We will strongly oppose the anti-European xenophobic right wing in any Euro referendum. But we oppose the 'stability pact' that the European Union seeks to impose on all those who join the euro. This pact would outlaw government deficit spending and reinforce the drive to privatise and deregulate the economy and we will therefore vote 'No' in any referendum on this issue.
- Support for the people of Palestine and opposition to the apartheid system that oppresses them.
- An end to the destruction of the environment by states and corporations for whom profit is more important than sustaining the natural world on which all life depends.

GIVE YOUR SUPPORT TO RESPECT!

☐ I'd like to join Respect and enclose £10 (£5 low- or unwaged), payable to **Respect Renewal Conference**

☐ I'd like to make a donation of £.............. payable to **Respect Renewal Conference**

☐ I'd like to offer my time and skills

☐ I would like further information

☐ I am a student/trade union member

NAME

ADDRESS

POSTCODE

EMAIL

COLLEGE/TRADE UNION

STANDING ORDER FORM
Please send to us at: Respect Renewal, PO Box 1109, London N4 2UU

I wish to take out a standing order for **Respect Renewal Conference** for [amount] £............. [amount in words] ....
First payment to be made on [date]...
and thereafter each month on the same day.
Bank name ....
Bank address ....
.... Post code ....
Account holder's name ....
Account number.. Sort code ....
Signature ....
Please pay to NATWEST BANK, sort code 60-80-08, account number 60601051, account name Respect Renewal Conference

SOCIALIST RESISTANCE PUBLICATIONS

Socialist Resistance is engaged in a programme of publishing a new range of books. Some are reprinted, with new introductions; others are new collections of writings on issues vital to the left today.
Shown here are:
Karl Kautsky's seminal analysis of the foundations of Christianity;
collected writings on ecosocialism, edited by Jane Kelly & Sheila Malone;
Ron Ridenour's sequel to his *Cuba at the Crossroads*;
a discussion with John Holloway's argument on state power, edited by Phil Hearse;
and a collection of writings on Israel, Palestine and the Middle East over a 60-year period, edited by Roland Rance and Terry Conway.

These can all be ordered from Socialist Resistance or online from Amazon (www.amazon.co.uk)

KARL KAUTSKY

FOUNDATIONS OF CHRISTIANITY

WITH ESSAYS BY MICHAEL LÖWY, DAVID PACKER, LIAM MAC UAID

ECOSOCIALISM

OR

BARBARISM

Edited by Jane Kelly and Sheila Malone

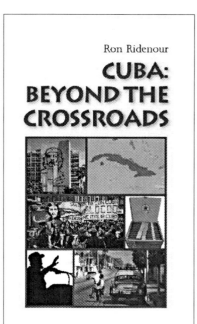

Ron Ridenour

CUBA: BEYOND THE CROSSROADS

TAKE THE POWER TO CHANGE THE WORLD

GLOBALISATION AND THE DEBATE ON POWER

Edited with an introduction by Phil Hearse

Middle East: war, imperialism, and ecology
Sixty years of resistance

PROMISED LAND
CLOSED

Edited by Roland Rance and Terry Conway

CONTACT US...

Send your form to:
Socialist Resistance
PO Box 1109
London N4 2UU

www.socialistresistance.net

You can also read
International Viewpoint
(journal of the Fourth
International) on the website:
www.internationalviewpoint.org

JOIN US...

If you are interested in the ideas in
this pamphlet, why not join Socialist
Resistance?

Please tick the box(es) and send this
form to our address on the left:

☐ I want a free information pack

☐ I want to be contacted by a
Socialist Resistance supporter in
my area

Name: [   ]

Adress: [   ]

eMail: [   ]

Phone: [   ]

Lightning Source UK Ltd.
Milton Keynes UK
UKOW02f1407190814

237168UK00001B/140/A